FOOD: TOO
TOO HI...

FOOD: TOO FADDY, TOO FAT

How to deal with your child's eating problems and enjoy mealtimes together

Dr John Pearce

Thorsons
An Imprint of HarperCollins Publishers

To Mary

Thorsons
An Imprint of Grafton Books
A Division of HarperCollins*Publishers*
77–85 Fulham Palace Road,
Hammersmith, London W6 8JB

Published by Thorsons 1991

1 3 5 7 9 10 8 6 4 2

© Dr John Pearce 1991

Dr John Pearce asserts the moral right to
be identified as the author of this work

British Library Cataloguing in Publication Data

Pearce, John *1940 Oct. 27-*
Food: too faddy too fat.
1. Children. Food habits. Nutritional aspects
I. Title
613.2088054

ISBN 0-7225-2283-4

Typeset by Harper Phototypesetters Limited,
Northampton, England
Printed and bound in Great Britain by
Collins Manufacturing, Glasgow

CONTENTS

INTRODUCTION

Eating and emotion are so closely tied together that food and love sometimes come to mean much the same thing. Parents may give a sweet or an ice cream to their child as a sign of caring, or a box of chocolates to each other as a sign of loving. Sometimes food and feelings go against each other, for example when somebody is so excited or upset that his or her appetite is lost.

However, although eating is so easily affected by feelings, it is in fact a very basic habit that is formed when children are still very young: the eating pattern is then set for the rest of that person's life. Naturally it is possible to have bad habits as well as good ones, and this book looks at how bad eating habits get started, what to do about them, and how they can be prevented.

Perhaps one of the most frustrating things for parents to cope with is when a child won't eat 'properly'. The child may be too fussy, or too greedy, or the table manners may be so bad that the meal is a misery. Whatever the problem, the mealtime is spoilt, and all the effort that went into making the food seems a waste of time and effort. What is particularly annoying is that if you get cross with a child at mealtimes it usually makes things even worse, while ignoring the problem won't improve things – either way it can be extremely upsetting.

This book is not particularly about difficult or disturbed

children. It is about 'normal' children and day-to-day eating problems that are not a major concern, but which nevertheless may take up a lot of your time and energy and which could even build up into a big problem if allowed to continue. Many of the eating problems of adults can be traced back to early childhood so it is best to sort things out early on rather than to wait and hope for the best. Try not to worry too much about any eating problems that your child may develop – the worry will upset your own appetite! In any case, there is a lot of that can be done, and the body has a remarkable way of adjusting to unusual food intake. It is only in extreme cases that eating problems can affect health.

You might ask, 'Why do parents need to read a book on children's eating? Surely it is better to follow your own instinct and do what comes naturally?' This approach still works for many parents, but nowadays instinct seems to be less reliable, perhaps because we have become too intellectual about bringing up children. Maybe there is too much advice, too many TV and radio programmes (and even too many books!) on bringing up children. Another factor is that more parents than ever before have to cope with the care of their children on their own (about 1 in 6 families at the last count). Also more families have both parents going out to work (about 60 per cent of families with school-age children). Both these factors make life more complicated for parents and give less time for working out how to solve any problems that do occur.

Over the past few years there have been great advances in the understanding of feeding and eating – why some children are too faddy and others are too fat and what can be done about it. But childcare is so easily influenced by fashions that parents often follow the latest trend without knowing what evidence there is to back it up. Unfortunately, completely up-to-date information is not easily available because it is published in many different scientific journals and even then the research is often contradictory.

The research on food allergies and difficult behaviour is a good example of this.

You may think that I sometimes take a rather firm line that could cause children to become upset, but if you read the book carefully you will find there is always a good reason for being tough. Please remember that being loving and being indulgent are not the same thing. Indeed, more trouble is caused by parents giving in 'for a quiet life' than for any other reason. It is not all that easy to stick to what you have said and to keep to what you believe is right, especially if you are not sure that you are doing the right thing in the first place. Children gain a great deal of security and comfort when their parents are prepared to be firm and give clear limits to behaviour in a consistent and caring way. In fact this is a good way of showing your love for your child.

I would like you to feel that I am talking directly to you as you read through the book. You can 'talk' back to me if you don't agree with what I have said or if you don't understand. Then read on and it should become clear why I have taken a certain line rather than any other. Don't hold back from having an argument with me in your head or asking other people what they think. In this way you will become much clearer about what you believe yourself.

Childcare is not so much about right and wrong, but more about finding the best compromise between the various demands of family life. For this reason it is impossible to 'get it right' all the time and, for parents, this often leads to feelings of guilt. In fact, a normal part of being a parent is feeling guilty about not always doing the right thing for your child!

If you are unsure about your own ideas, but have some reservations about what I have written, I would like you to follow my suggestions as closely as possible, in spite of any reservations you might have. I have been very careful to give guidelines and advice only where I am confident that they are safe, reasonable, and effective. If you have followed the guidelines carefully and they have still not worked, please don't immediately think that I have got it all wrong. It is much more likely that you haven't been sticking closely enough to what I have said. So read the book again, have another go . . . and don't give up!

It is the love you have for your child that makes being a parent so fulfilling and full of joy. But it is the same bond of affection that makes it so painful and distressing when things go wrong. Our feelings of love vary from time to time and fortunately it isn't necessary to love your child all the time in order to be a reasonable parent.

CHAPTER 1

EARLY FEEDING PROBLEMS

Feeding and Feelings

The link between food and emotion is incredibly close. It starts as soon as a baby is born. Breast feeding causes warm and caring feelings in mothers and fathers as well. But these strong positive feelings can easily turn into distress and anxiety if there are any problems with the feeding. Exactly the same applies to bottle feeding, although the emotions may not be as strong because bottle feeding isn't quite so personal as breast feeding.

If a baby rejects the milk by crying, being sick, or just drifting off to sleep, it is very difficult not to take it personally and feel that you must be doing something wrong. Not surprisingly this is very upsetting and so parents desperately try to think what on earth the cause could be and what they can do to make things better. For example they might:

- change the milk
- bring the wind up
- rock the baby
- change the nappy
- add some solids
- give more milk
- walk around holding the baby

- **feed more often**
- **change the size of the teat hole**

Usually one or other of these changes will make all the difference and you can relax again. However, it is often more by chance rather than for any other reason that things get better. Unfortunately, worries about feeding are catching and can be picked up by your baby, so taking a more relaxed attitude to feeding problems is one of the most helpful things that any parent can do. Now that is the difficult bit and is easier said than done! How is it possible to be relaxed when your baby refuses food or has sicked the meal up again?

Taking Advice

All the books on babycare have many pages on these early feeding problems and give lots of advice for worried parents. In fact, lack of advice is rarely a problem at this stage. Parents usually have much *too much* advice in the first few months after the baby is born. Unfortunately much of this early advice is contradictory. Grannies, mothers-in-law, neighbours, health visitors, GPs, magazines, and all the rest often disagree with each other about what is best to do. Here are some guidelines that may help you to make up your mind when the experts disagree:

- **Of all the people giving advice, whom do you trust the most? Think about their advice first. There is no point in following the advice of somebody you don't trust.**
- **Does this advice feel right to you? Are you reasonably comfortable with it? Only try something that makes some sense to you.**
- **Only try one approach at a time.**
- **Give enough time for the new method to work.**

Most new approaches take at least two weeks to work.
- **Don't be half-hearted about the method you are using. Do it properly, and if in doubt go back to the person who gave you the advice.**
- **Watch out for your own worries and lack of confidence getting in the way. Small children pick up their parents' worries so very easily and this only makes things worse. Don't hesitate to ask for help when things are difficult.**

Because there is so much advice available on feeding babies I shall only deal with those aspects of early feeding that are useful to know about in order to understand the problems that may occur later. Advice on early feeding goes through fashions where the type of milk or timing of feeding changes. How can parents sort out all this muddle and decide what is the best? Perhaps you should be reassured by the fact that there isn't any agreement – because this usually means that it probably doesn't matter too much what you do!

Milk – Breast and Bottle

Type of Milk

Breast milk is of course specially suited for babies, but occasionally it can cause problems if the mother is taking any form of drug or food that the baby could react to. For example, medicine to help the mother sleep will also make the baby sleepy because some of the medicine will be in the milk. Alcohol may cause similar problems. Allergic reactions to breast milk itself are virtually unheard of, although they can occur. More often babies react to foods or drinks that the mother has taken which then come out in the milk.

Allergic responses to cows' milk may occur in infancy,

but are more obvious in toddlers. Allergy to milk can result in a rash, diarrhoea, poor feeding, tummy aches, and even blood in the stools. The trouble is that these symptoms are not all that unusual and can be due to many other causes apart from milk allergy.

Unfortunately, skin tests for milk allergy may not be very helpful because many children will show a positive skin reaction in spite of having no obvious signs of allergy to milk. The best way to test for cows' milk allergy is to stop all milk and dairy foods (for no longer than 3–4 days), giving goats' or soya milk instead (remember that allergic reactions are also possible to these other types of milk). If there is an allergy to cows' milk, you can expect to see a dramatic improvement in the symptoms. If this is the case, you should then get more detailed advice from a dietitian or your GP on how to provide a suitable diet for your child.

Breast milk is relatively low in protein which means that breast fed babies are less likely to go for more than 2-3 hours between feeds without waking and crying. The higher level of protein in cows' milk allows babies to go for longer between feeds. Another interesting finding is that the composition of breast milk changes towards the end of each feed. The fat content increases and this may well act as a signal to the baby that the feed is coming to an end. Bottle fed babies will not have this signal from the milk and will therefore tend to carry on and on . . .

If you think that there is a problem with the milk, it is best to get advice from a doctor or health visitor before changing to another type of milk. It is very easy to get into a muddle by chopping and changing, when perhaps there was no problem with the milk in the first place. If possible it is best to continue breast feeding for at least the first 3 months, because the milk contains antibodies that help protect the baby against infections until it has started to develop its own immunity. In addition it has been sug-gested that the relatively high fat content of breast milk is helpful in the production of the insulating fatty layer around nerves that makes them work more efficiently.

The Teat

Teats, nipples, and babies' mouths come in all shapes and sizes, so it is not surprizing that they don't always fit together well. A lot can be done – even changing the shape of nipples is possible! The midwife or health visitor should be able to help you with advice about this.

For bottle fed babies it is important to get the size of the hole in the teat just right so that the feed doesn't go on too long with a hole that is too small and the baby doesn't choke because the hole is too big. The only way of doing this is to experiment, but if you are going to breast feed as well as using the bottle, it is best to keep the hole on the small side so that the baby doesn't get lazy about sucking and give up when put to the breast.

The Temperature

Milk at body temperature goes down the best. However, as the child grows older and starts to take solids and to drink from a cup, it is a good idea to vary the temperature a bit and to offer slightly colder foods so that the child eventually gets used to eating things at room temperature. Otherwise it is easy to find yourself having to warm everything up for your child and making life unnecessarily complicated.

Weaning

It used to be fashionable to introduce solid foods as early as the first few weeks of life in a very soft and sloppy form. This seemed to stop babies crying and so it was assumed to be a good thing. However, crying is a normal way for babies to communicate and express themselves and it may not mean that anything is seriously wrong (see my book *Worries and Fears* in this series). In general babies are not ready to eat solid food until their teeth start to appear at around 6 months old, although it is reasonable to start introducing semi-solid food from 3 months old. However, recently there has been some suggestion that early weaning is linked with later food intolerance, especially to wheat products such as bread, rusks, and biscuits. It is therefore best to wean on rice, fruit and vegetables.

Many babies reject solid food when it is first offered and it is important not to take this personally. There is no need to panic! Just make the food a bit softer and take it slowly step by step. Start with food that you know your child likes and only try giving it when you know that he or she is hungry. If that doesn't work, give it a rest for a few days and then try again later – there is plenty of time. One point to remember is that as you increase solids the baby will not need quite so much milk, otherwise weight gain may be too fast.

Learning to Drink and Eat

Drinking and eating are such normal activities that we don't stop to think about them. In fact they are very complicated processes. Many different muscles and nerves have to work together in exactly the right way in order for us to be able to swallow without choking. For the first six months or so after birth, eating solid food is just too difficult and the baby only learns how to do this very gradually. Fortunately babies are born with a number of inbuilt reflexes that come into action automatically to help with drinking. There is a head turning reflex that causes the baby's head to turn to one side if the cheek on the same side is touched lightly. This means that the baby will naturally face towards the breast when being fed. If the baby's lips or side of the mouth are touched, the mouth will open and then if something is put gently into the mouth the baby will automatically start to suck and to swallow.

In addition to these complicated reflexes that make drinking possible there are automatic protective reflexes that stop food and fluid going the wrong way and possibly ending up in the lungs. One of these safety reflexes is called the 'gag reflex' which is caused by anything hard or unusual making contact with the back of the throat. This then closes off the throat to block the passage of food. The gag reflex may cause difficulty with feeding if the spoon or teat is put too far into the baby's mouth. It can also occur if the food is too hard or the wrong temperature.

It obviously helps to know about these basic reflexes if you are having problems feeding your baby. For example, all reflexes are usually less well established in premature or ill babies. Occasionally the reflexes are weak and poorly co-ordinated in babies who are quite normal in other ways (these children sometimes have speech and other co-ordination problems later on). Babies are born with a very powerful sucking reflex needed to get milk from the breast, but much less effort is required with a bottle. So once a bottle has been used, it may be difficult to get babies to suck at the breast again, unless they are really hungry.

Not surprsingly, the reflexes and co-ordination required for eating solid food are even more complex than those needed for coping with fluids. These reflexes develop over the first few months of life and are normally ready to cope with solid food when the first teeth appear. There is some evidence to suggest that if solid foods are not started within the first year, then children may find it difficult to establish the necessary co-ordination to deal with solid food, resulting in a whole new set of feeding problems.

Feeding a tiny baby in the first few months of life can be worrying if you haven't done it before. It helps to remember that all these amazing reflexes are working together to help you to feed your baby. What is more, there are also reflexes that occur in a mother that help with feeding. For example, the flow of the mother's milk is increased when the baby touches the breast or cries. Also, the more that the breast is emptied of milk the better it fills up again, which is why it is best to express any remaining milk after a feed. However, if the breast becomes too full or engorged with milk, this is likely to reduce milk production.

In spite of all the help from natural reflexes, feeding can be very difficult if the baby refuses to drink or regurgitates the food. I shall now look at some common early feeding problems, first those caused by the baby, then those which are due to the parent!

Feeding Problems Due to the Baby

Prematurity

The more premature a baby is, the more difficulty it will have with feeding, because the necessary reflexes are still being developed. If, for example, a baby is born a month early, you might expect the feeding to be a problem until 4 weeks of age. If the baby is more than 6 weeks early, it may be necessary to give the feeds by tube for a short time. Vomiting and regurgitation of feeds is very common indeed in premature babies and a great deal of time and skill is usually needed to get through those first few weeks. It can be a very demanding time for all those concerned. However, there is no reason why any feeding problems should continue after those first few weeks unless there are some other causes at work.

There is of course nothing much that can be done about prematurity, but smaller amounts of feed given more frequently may help. Some babies may need to be fed every 2 hours at first.

Vomiting and Regurgitating

The valve at the bottom of the tube (the oesophegus) that

leads from the mouth to the stomach is not fully formed in babies and as a result they bring up food rather easily. This tendency diminishes naturally as babies grow bigger, but while it lasts it can cause a lot of worry and distress. It is not at all unusual for a baby to have just finished a feed and then to regurgitate what seems like most of the meal. This is often not as bad as it seems. A little milk goes a long way. To get an idea of how much of the feed has been brought up you could try spilling some milk or water on purpose in order to help you estimate how much has come up (no need to do this every time of course!).

If regurgitation is a problem, then feeding smaller amounts more frequently and winding more frequently may help. It may also help to keep the baby propped up after meals. Specialist help will be needed if the problem continues. If the vomiting produces large amounts and is very forceful, it is best to ask for professional advice from your health visitor or doctor at the first opportunity.

'Wind'

A full stomach due to either food or wind or both will cause a baby to be less keen to suck, and if the stomach is very

distended it may lead to crying. Wind in the stomach gets blamed for more than its fair share of crying, but at least it is a simple and safe problem that is relatively easy to deal with. There is no right or wrong way of dealing with wind – what works for your baby is the best. Sitting the baby upright, leaning slightly forwards with its chin up is a good position. It is possible to get some idea of how much wind there is in the stomach by giving the tummy a light flick with the finger and listening to the sound it makes. You will soon come to recognize the hollow sound of a windy stomach.

Illness

Any form of illness can put a baby off its food in the same way that we lose our appetite when we are ill. Even a minor problem like a blocked nose or sore throat can make feeding difficult. Until a child has learnt to talk it can be quite difficult to tell when he or she is feeling unwell, and so not feeding properly can be a very useful sign that something is wrong. An equally helpful sign of illness is when a previously active baby becomes lethargic and floppy.

Don't expect your child to eat properly until the illness has completely gone. Sick children require normal amounts of fluid (the fluids can be increased if the temperature is raised), so keep the fluids going even if you stop giving solid food.

Tiredness

Small babies sleep more than they are awake and it isn't at all unusual for it to be necessary to wake a baby up for a feed or even during a feed. Very young babies tend to 'cat nap' – with periods of sleep lasting 20 minutes or so, alternating with short periods of wakefulness. So you can see that if a baby's feed takes longer than half an hour, it would not be at all surprising if the baby goes off to sleep while still drinking. It is therefore important to keep the baby awake and to keep it busy drinking during feeding times: it may help to give smaller feeds more frequently.

Discomfort

Not surprisingly any pain or discomfort will interfere with feeding. This could even include rather mild things like bright lights or loud noises. A full nappy or a sore rash (such as thrust infection of the mouth or bottom) are also common causes of distraction from feeding. Pain and discomfort is very difficult to assess in babies because they can't talk and in any case they cry a lot even when there is nothing much wrong with them.

It is normally possible for most parents to recognize a different type of crying that is higher pitched and more urgent than usual which indicates pain or distress. Feeding will return to normal as soon as the cause of the distress has been sorted out. It is always a good idea to feed your child in a fairly quiet, warm, and relaxed atmosphere, away from bright lights, loud sounds, and the distractions of radio and TV.

Obstructions

Very rarely babies are born with a blockage or narrowing in the food passage. This type of problem is easy to notice very soon after birth. The signs are fairly obvious with vomiting and/or nothing being passed downwards – so no motions or wind. Congenital blockage (atresia) can be expected to show up in the first week of life, but some conditions like pyloric stenosis (a blocked outlet from the stomach) develop after 2-8 weeks without any earlier problems, resulting in a clear change from the normal feeding pattern and in 'projectile' vomiting that comes shooting out under high pressure. One of the conditions that can occasionally cause a rather sudden blockage of the intestine in the first few years of life is called intussusception. Here the bowel folds back on itself and causes pain, bleeding from the rectum, constipation, and vomiting.

These conditions are quite rare so there is no need to worry about them each time your child is sick. I have mentioned them only so that you know what symptoms to look out for. Apart from excessive vomiting and constipation the other general signs of blockage include a bulging out of the tummy and pain. If in any doubt you should get a medical opinion.

Nerves and Muscles

Sometimes children are born with throat and mouth muscles and/or nerves that don't work properly together. One example would be where the 'gag reflex' (described above) is weak and results in food going the wrong way and choking the child.

This type of problem is usually very difficult to diagnose, so specialist help may be required from a paediatrician. Fortunately these conditions can be expected to improve with time. In the meantime great care has to be taken with feeding and it is usually necessary to give fluid feeds for much longer than normal.

Temperament

Some babies are born with a difficult temperament and so the problems start right from the very beginning. These children cry a great deal, they are slow to settle after any change, but most importantly from the point of view of feeding problems, they are very unpredictable with eating. Sometimes there will be little or no problem, but on other occasions mealtimes will be marked by food refusal.

Children with a difficult temperament need 'super parenting' with more regularity and routine than normal. They also benefit from extra firmness and caring, together with very clear limits set for their behaviour, so that they know exactly how far they can go.

Feeding Problems Due to Parents

Babies and young children can be difficult to feed, but parents may also be the cause of some of the problems, even though they are doing their best. It is possible for parents to try too hard to get the feeding right, with the result that meals become times for tension and stress.

Lack of Experience

Parents have to learn on the job with the first child, and to some extent use the child as an experimental guinea pig, learning by trial and error. There is no way round this, so

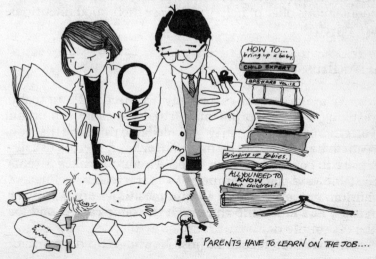

PARENTS HAVE TO LEARN ON THE JOB....

don't feel bad about asking for extra help and support. In fact first born children don't do so badly – there is some evidence to suggest that eldest children achieve more academically and are more responsible than children in other positions in the family!

As a first-time parent it is so easy to be muddled by all the contradictory advice, so check out the guidelines again on pages 11-12 before deciding what to do. Above all don't feel guilty if you find the baby is difficult to feed – almost all parents have these feelings at one time or another.

Illness

Any form of physical or psychological illness can lead to problems with feeding because the parent's patience and energy will be in short supply. It is very easy, particularly if you are a mother, to push yourself to carry on even if you are too ill to cope. Try and remember that by neglecting your own needs you will not be able to do the best for your child. Ask for help earlier rather than later. Most people will be keen to give you help, but may hesitate to make a spontaneous offer of help just in case their good intentions are rejected.

Tiredness

Many parents become chronically overtired without really realizing what the problem is. Tiredness can creep up on you gradually and you may be fooled into thinking that you seem to be coping and getting by. However, there is usually a price to pay for being overtired. Tiredness makes parents irritable and short tempered and increases feelings of tension and anxiety – very soon mealtimes are no longer relaxed and enjoyable and much the same can be said for the rest of the day.

You may not recognize just how overtired you have

YOU MAY NOT RECOGNISE JUST **HOW TIRED** YOU HAVE BECOME....

become. If there is any doubt, it is worthwhile organizing a few good nights' sleep to see if it makes any difference to how you feel.

Worries

Tension and anxieties are easily picked up by babies and young children because they are so physically and emotionally close to their parents at that age. However hard you try, it is going to be virtually impossible to hide your feelings. Don't be surprised if your child picks up how you feel and starts showing the same emotions – it is all very normal. Feelings are 'infectious' and worries are the most catching of all emotions. Unfortunately tension and anxiety affect the appetite and interfere with normal eating. The chances are that if your anxiety is the cause of your baby not eating properly, then you will also have eating problems yourself.

The most important thing is to be aware of any upsetting

emotions that are around and to deal with them if possible. Try and avoid the vicious cycle of worrying about the worry that your child may have picked up from you.

Conclusions

You can see that most of the reasons for feeding difficulties are shared by parents and babies. A vicious cycle can easily develop in which one problem contributes to the other. For example, a tired, overworked mother may not have the extra time and perseverance that a premature or sick baby requires. The result is that the baby cries and won't feed properly. The mother then becomes even more tired and upset and so it goes on. Don't hesitate to ask for help at an early stage, before problems develop.

This book is not about the more specialized problems of early feeding difficulties because these need to be sorted out on an individual basis. I have given some general background details that will tie in with other parts of the book and help in the understanding of feeding problems later on in childhood. If you need more specific help with baby feeding problems, there are a lot of books on this topic and many people to help and advise you.

CHAPTER 2

TOO FADDY

Faddy Children Are Made, Not Born

Almost all of us have some food or other that we avoid if possible. Even the thought of the food may be enough to make us feel ill. Just try thinking about eating raw fish eyes! The foods that we like and don't like have a lot to do with habits and expectations. If, when you were very young, you had been told that a dish of raw fish eyes, with cold cooked cabbage, is really wonderful, but you were allowed to have it only on special occasions, you would probably come to think of it as a great delicacy, worth paying a lot for.

There is an important message here. Most of the food fads that children have are picked up from the attitude or example of other people. Food fads are rarely due to deep inborn dislikes that are present at birth and which never change for the rest of time. The fads are most frequently due to social customs and habits. However, children are sometimes allergic to certain foods and eating them will cause symptoms such as tummy ache or some other feeling of being unwell. These unpleasant symptoms will always occur after eating the food, usually within 24 hours. Not surprisingly children who are allergic to a particular food won't enjoy eating it.

Very young children tend not to like strong tastes or

smells of any kind and most children will show a preference for some foods rather than others from an early age. Although likes and dislikes naturally change with time, once a particular dislike of a food has gone on for several years it may well become fixed and then very difficult to change.

How Food Fads Are Made

The normal likes and dislikes of children for various foods develop from a very early age. Most babies object to any change in their milk and are not keen to accept more solid food when it is first offered to them. It is not difficult to see how a baby who spits out solid food could be thought to dislike it or even to be allergic to it. How parents react to this early rejection of food is critical because it sets the scene for later food fads.

If parents think – or say – any of the following things too often, then strong food likes and dislikes will soon develop:

- 'Oh dear, is my food upsetting you?'
- 'I will give you whatever food you want to make you happy'
- 'I get upset when you don't like my food'
- 'I worry about your health if you don't eat everything that I give you'
- 'I worry about you losing weight'
- 'You must eat more . . . or else!'
- 'If you don't eat properly I will be cross'
- 'Here is some food that you like to keep you quiet'

These reactions to children being fussy about food are quite normal. We alll do it and problems are only likely to develop if these responses are repeated over and over again. Children soon realize that how and when they eat food has a powerful effect on other people. Even very young babies

BABIES FIND THAT THEY CAN **INFLUENCE** WHAT THEIR PARENTS DO....

become aware of this ability to use food to influence their parents – perhaps this is because they are so in tune with their parents' emotions at that stage of development.

As soon as babies find that they can influence what their parents do, they quickly learn how to use this to get their own way. This may sound as though babies are rather nasty manipulative little thugs, but this is not really how it is. Nature has made it so that even tiny babies can have some effect on the world around them and make their needs known. Our problem is to understand the message that the baby is trying to get across. What does it mean if the baby refuses to take more than half the feed or spits food out?

Obviously it takes a combination of intuition and common sense to work out what is going on. If you are still not sure, it may help to ask yourself the following questions:

- 'Is there something wrong with the food?'
- 'Is there something wrong with my child?'
- 'Is there something wrong with me?'

If there is nothing wrong then maybe your child has found that rejecting food is a very good way of getting extra care and attention. Just think of the high level of attention babies have during their feeding times in the first few weeks after birth. Sooner or later this has to change because there are other things that have to be done. But children quickly discover that the attention comes back to them if they are difficult with their food. If this goes on for a year or two, your child will have had a lot of practice in rejecting food and will eventually turn into a fussy and faddy eater.

What is Wrong with Being Faddy?

Why shouldn't children decide for themselves what food they would like to eat? Perhaps we should allow children to eat whatever they like, even if this means living on only two or three foods. Certainly it is possible to live on milk alone for a long time with no serious problems. Babies do it – so why shouldn't children? Some children seem to manage well on a very limited range of foods, such as crisps, sausages, chocolate, and fizzy drinks! Does this matter?

Fortunately our bodies have an amazing ability to get the nutrients out of any food, so it is possible to survive quite well on what might seem to be a very restricted diet. In some ways this should reassure parents who have a fussy child, but there are a range of possible problems that may occur as a result of allowing a child to remain faddy for a long time. Fussy children are likely to have one or more of the following problems. They may:

- **develop vitamin deficiencies**
- **miss out on essential nutrients**
- **grow rather slowly**
- **be difficult and stubborn about other things**
- **have a lower resistance to stress**
- **be socially embarrassing when eating out**
- **feel socially embarrassed as a teenager**

- make life more difficult for themselves
- make life more difficult for their families

This is quite a long list and, as can be seen, both the physical and the psychological well-being of the child can be affected. There are long term effects as well as short term and both the child and other people may be affected by the child's fussiness. Food fads can be survived, but at a cost. So they are best avoided if possible.

Preventing Food Fads

Once it is understood that food fads can develop as a result of a child using rejection of food to gain attention, it is not too difficult to work out what can be done to prevent them occurring in the first place. Food must not be allowed to be used regularly as a method of communicating with and controlling other people. Here are some examples of how parents and their children use food as a form of communication and a way of controlling each other:

The Parent Controls the Child

- 'If you're good I'll give you a sweet'
- 'You will have to sit there until you've eaten it all up'
- 'I'll give you extra food so that you will know that I love you'
- 'Please, please eat it up or I'll be upset'
- 'I'm so cross with you that I won't give you any tea'

The Child Controls the Parent

- 'I'm angry with you so I won't eat up all my dinner'
- 'I think I'll eat very slowly to get your attention'

- 'I'll upset you by refusing to eat properly'
- 'You can't make me eat it, I am more stubborn than you'
- 'I'll make you happy by eating everything you give me and more, even if this means I will grow fat'

In most cases food fads develop from a combination of two main factors working together:

- The natural tendency to dislike any new food that is different in texture, taste, smell, or appearance
- The food becoming the 'message' or the 'weapon' to be used as a way of communicating between the parent and the child

This is a very normal process that occurs with every child at some stage. How parents respond to this situation will to a large extent determine how fussy the child is. But it is more complicated than this because there are other factors to take into account, such as:

- *Food allergies*. One of the most common allergies is due to cows' milk, but many other foods and some additives may cause an allergic reaction which in turn may be the reason that the child doesn't like a particular food.
- *Difficult temperament*. Some children are born with a difficult temperament. Typically they are unpredictable and give problems with feeding right from the start. They also cry excessively and don't react well to any change of food.
- *Family food fads*. Many families have a range of foods that they avoid as a result of moral, cultural, or traditional reasons. These are easily passed onto the children.
- *Parental attitude*. Parents differ a lot on how they deal with fussiness. Being very strict and making

"and to my great-nephew Tom, I bequeath my lifetime FIRM DISLIKE OF BOILED PARSNIPS...."

children eat everything up may cause food dislikes, but even more likely to do so is being very soft and indulgent.

- *Stubborn personality*. This is not quite the same as the difficult temperament which is made up from a typical pattern of characteristics. Stubbornness may occur as an isolated personality feature and is very similar to being single-minded and self-willed. Stubborn children can dig their feet in like a donkey and resist all persuasion. In fact, the harder you try to change them the more they dig in and stick where they are.
- *Food cults*. There are a number of accepted food avoidance groups such as vegetarians, lacto-vegetarians, and vegans.

What practical steps can parents take to help their child avoid permanent food fads? Well, before doing anything at all it is important to decide where you stand with food fads. There are so many things that a parent has to worry about. Is it really worth all the upset of yet another worry? Although faddiness can cause problems, it isn't that serious when compared with something like disobedience. In any case it would seem quite reasonable to allow children at least one or two foods that they are allowed to avoid – after all most adults have their own hated food that they can't stand. However, if you have decided that you would like to encourage your child to be *less fussy* with food then here are some step-by-step guidelines to help you.

General Guidelines and Two Approaches

- **Make sure that everybody who looks after your child agrees about what food can and can't be avoided. You won't make much progress if you can't agree.**
- **It is usually easier to deal with one food fad at a time, rather than trying to get your child to eat everything.**
- **Remember that your child has the final say in what he or she eats.**
- **There is no way you can force people to eat something against their will short of tube feeding, and even then they can always sick it up again!**
- **Be sure that you show no sign of worry or distress about the feeding, otherwise your fussy child will soon learn how to wind you up by refusing food and then use this as way of controlling you and communicating with you.**
- **There are two main ways of dealing with this problem. There is the '*in at the deep end*' approach that may cause some distress, but is over and done with quickly and any upset is short-lived, causing no lasting problems. Then there is the '*slowly slowly, bit by bit*' approach. This can take ages and lots of determination. There is little or no distress with this method but the issue goes on and on and may get in the way of other things that you would like to deal with.**

- **Avoid snacks between meals if you want your child to have a good appetite for the next meal.**
- **Finally, don't forget to avoid battles about food. There is no way that you can win.**

The 'In At The Deep End' Approach

Just as some children learn to swim by going straight in at the deep end of the pool, so do a few children overcome food fads because they absolutely *have* to eat a disliked food, for example when eating at a friend's house. If you want to help your fussy child in this way, you will need to persuade the child that it is much quicker to do it this way. However, if normal persuasion and reasoning don't work, then there isn't much point going on and on about it. You know yourself that the longer you stand on the edge of a swimming pool filled with icy cold water the more difficult it is to take the plunge and the more likely you are to go and find something better to do. Trying to eat a food you really don't like is just like that. The 'in at the deep end' approach would operate in a step-by-step way something like this:

- **You know which foods your child doesn't like.**
- **You decide which foods you expect your child to eat.**
- **You give the foods in amounts that you think are reasonable.**
- **You expect all the food that you provide to be eaten up.**
- **If the disliked food is left on the plate and not eaten, no further food is given for that meal, on the assumption that the child can't be hungry.**
- **If the food is left it is usually best to make it into soup or give it to the cat, but if you want to be really tough you could offer it again for the next meal. Remember not to give snacks between meals, otherwise the child won't be hungry.**

- It helps to organize meals so that favourite foods are served after disliked foods. Naturally they are only offered if the disliked food is eaten up.
- If in spite of all your efforts the food fad remains, don't worry. Have a rest and don't bother to get upset – it isn't that important. Just try again after a few weeks and remember that you have a 'trump card'!

Your Trump Card – A Secret Weapon!

We are all born with a number of instinctual drives that are necessary for life to continue and consist of an irresistible urge to have a need met. The drives that are immediately necessary for life to continue are called primary drives, those that are important but less vital on a daily basis are called secondary drives, and finally there are tertiary drives that are necessary for life in a much broader sense.

You might think of other drives or put them in a different order, but these are generally accepted to be the most important ones. Freud built his theory of the mind with the assumption that sex was a primary drive and a powerful motivator for our thoughts and behaviour, but most people would now agree that there are other drives that are much more relevant to normal everyday life.

Eating is a primary drive that shows itself as appetite and hunger. Primary drives are very strong and can't be resisted for very long under normal circumstances. This is your trump card.

It is possible to go without food for many hours, but the body can't last for more than a few hours without fluid. As a rough guide, it is possible for children to go without food for 10 hours for every year of life up to 5 years old without any problem, (ie. 10 hours for a 1 year old, 20 hours for a 2 year old, up to 50 hours for anyone 5 years or older), *provided that fluid intake is adequate*. This may sound rather tough, but remember the treatment for any diarrhoea or vomiting is to stop all solid food and to give fluids only and this may have to go on for two or more days before the child recovers.

After a few hours on fluids only, most children will have developed a very good appetite and will eat things that they wouldn't have dreamed of eating a few hours earlier. So your trump card or secret weapon to deal with your child's eating problem is the primary drive of hunger. Sounds easy doesn't it? Unfortunately it isn't quite so simple, and it can only be used occasionally. There are also some important rules for safety if you are going to use hunger to increase your child's appetite.

Primary Drives – Immediately necessary for life to continue

> Breathing
> Eating
> Sleeping
> Drinking

Secondary Drives – Necessary for normal every-day life to continue

> Bodily comfort
> Caring, loving relationship
> Mental stimulation
> Praise and attention

Tertiary Drives – Necessary for humanity as a whole to continue

> Beauty
> Order and predictability
> Challenge and change
> Sexual satisfaction

Guidelines for Using Hunger Safely:

- *This approach can't be used on children who are underweight or ill* – if you have any doubts about it, ask your GP.
- *Never use hunger as a punishment* – not only is this unreasonable but it is potentially dangerous, because your child will come to think that food can be used as a way of being angry with people. Punishing a child by withholding one of the basic requirements of life is unacceptable and will surely make food and mealtimes into a battleground sooner or later.
- *Always give normal amounts of fluids to drink* – this is very important because the waste products of the body have to be got rid of and the kidneys must be kept going.
- *Remember that milk drinks are like food* – it is possible to live on milk alone, so you should treat it and other milky drinks as being the same as food.
- *Give water or low calorie drinks only between meals* – otherwise the child won't feel hungry.
- *Don't try this for longer than the times given above* – the body starts to run out of the normal food reserves and begins to breakdown body protein after a day or two without food.
- *Only use this approach if you feel it is the right thing to do* – if you are not reasonably confident about it, your child will quickly pick this up and do everything possible to make you feel bad.
- *Carefully plan out in advance how you are going to manage things* – the adults at home must agree and support the plan. Work out how long you feel it is reasonable to stick it out and what you are going to do at each point where things might go wrong. It may help to link this plan with some other activity, such as going out for the day so that

not having food will be less of an issue.
- *Some children lose their appetite as a result of under eating and being constantly underweight –* these children need to be brought up to normal weight before using hunger to get them to eat. This can be done by adding high calorie supplements to each meal.
- *Stay cool!* – if at any time you find that you are feeling upset about using hunger to increase your child's appetite, you can always stop and try again some other time.

In practice it is only reasonable to withhold food as part of a carefully worked out plan to help your own child. In other words it can only be done in the context of a loving family, carefully following the guidelines. Helping your child to be able to eat a wide range of healthy foods is one way of showing your feelings of love and care for your child.

The 'Slowly Slowly, Bit by Bit' Approach

The rather tough way of dealing with food fads described above, using hunger, will not suit everyone and much the same results can be achieved by taking it very slowly over many months or even years. The only problem is that you have to be very patient and avoid the big risk of having tense mealtimes hoping that your child won't notice the tiny bit of hated food that you have hidden away on the plate.

The aim with the slow and gradual method is to give your child very small portions of the disliked food, either hidden and mixed in with other food, or on its own but in such small quantities that it would be difficult to object. This is the way that most parents use to introduce new foods, so we know it works, but it can take ages. The danger is that it is very easy to become upset if it doesn't work quickly and

DISTRACTING YOUR CHILD....

then to give up altogether. Remember, it may take years!

If you find yourself becoming worked up and tense whenever your child refuses to eat something, you will need to find some way of coping with this, such as:

- **distracting yourself or your child**
- **not taking it personally**
- **planning what to do next time**
- **finding an excuse to leave the room for a short time until you have calmed down**

You will remember that food and feelings go hand in hand, so don't be surprised to find that you become emotional about food at times. This is quite normal, but control it if you can. Sometimes it helps to say something to defuse any tension that has built up. For example you could say:

- **'It doesn't worry me if you don't eat it now . . . you can have it later'**

- 'I am glad you don't like it . . . there will be more for me'
- 'I didn't think you would like it . . . you are not old enough for it yet'

Deliberate Vomiting

The fight over food is one that is best avoided and the most important reason of all is that it is a battle that you can't win. You may have managed to force feed your child using either physical strength or emotional blackmail, but this will only make the next meal more likely to be tense and difficult and all your hard work can be undone in a few minutes with your child performing the quick-sick routine. This is a child's ultimate weapon in the fight over food – bringing it back!

Some children find it much easier than others to be sick. In babies and young children the valve at the end of the tube to the stomach makes it very easy for food to come up, but by the end of the first year most children are only rarely sick. If you have one of those children that continues to vomit easily there are a few things that you can do to make things easier, such as:

- give smaller meals more frequently
- experiment with different foods
- make the food as solid as possible (there is a special additive to help you with this – ask your doctor)
- avoid drinks with the meal
- wait for an hour after meals before giving any drinks

One danger to look out for is where your child learns that being sick is a very good way of either making you upset or getting your attention – or both. You will know if this has happened because the vomiting occurs at times when your child is angry with you or when you are less able to give attention. If you think your child is indeed bringing food up to upset you or to gain your attention then the following ideas should make the vomiting less likely to happen:

- **Don't be upset! This is easier said than done, but nevertheless important.**
- **Try dealing with the vomiting as if your child had spilt some milk.**
- **Clear up the mess quickly, with the minimum of fuss.**
- **An older child might help with the clearing up.**
- **It may be best to say nothing at all – just clean up the sick.**
- **If you think your child is being sick to gain attention, try leaving the room for a few minutes at the first sign of vomiting.**

Obviously, you will need to be reassured that there is no serious physical cause for the sickness. It is usually fairly clear what is going on, but if you have any doubt it is best to consult your doctor.

What Happens to Faddy Children?

Food fads are very common in early childhood, but fade away as children grow older until in adult life most of us have only one or two foods that we can't stand. Fussiness about food therefore tends to get better on its own. It may well be that parents can actually keep food fads going by making them an issue or by saying things like:

- **'He won't eat carrots.'**
- **'You don't like fish, do you dear?'**
- **'I can't get her to eat cabbage.'**
- **'You are just as fussy as your grandfather.'**
- **'He never eats boiled eggs.'**

● 'There is no point in giving her custard, she won't eat it.'

Each of these statements is a negative one and gives the impression that there is no hope of improvement. At the same time the statements almost sound like an instruction to the child to remain fussy and keep the food fad.

Children with a stubborn nature who also have food fads are more likely than other children to get stuck and remain fussy, especially if eating has become a bit of a battle. A few

but we cannot go to the shops yet... you have a small ladder in your tights, Mother....

PEOPLE WHO BECOME FUSSY ABOUT THE **SMALL DETAILS** OF LIFE MAY BE VERY USEFUL BUT THEY CAN ALSO BE **VERY ANNOYING....**

faddy children will grow up into faddy adults which can make life difficult for anyone else preparing meals. Sometimes the fussiness can spread into other areas of everyday life and become part of a fussy personality with strong likes and dislikes. People who become fussy about the small details of life may be very useful, but they can also be very annoying.

Conclusions

Food fads are one of those everyday problems of childhood where making an issue out of it can make things worse, but doing nothing can cause difficulties later on. All parents have to decide what they think is reasonable and how many fussy food fads they are going to allow. The aim is to make mealtimes an enjoyable experience for everyone rather than a battleground with winners and losers. Once you have decided and agreed what your child should and shouldn't eat, it is important to remain determined and confident that you can achieve this using the approaches outlined above.

CHAPTER 3

TOO FAT

Chubby children are often described as looking healthy or 'bonny', but there comes a stage when being overweight becomes unhealthy and even dangerous. There is, however, very little agreement about how much weight is too much. One major problem in deciding if a child is too fat is that it is normal to put on weight during childhood, we would worry if this didn't happen, and in any case it is quite normal for children to pass through phases of being a bit overweight.

A child's weight is a focus of parents' concern right from the birth – if not before – the main worry being that not enough weight is being put on. It is therefore hardly surprising that some children become first chubby and then positively fat. Children grow and develop gradually and it is often more difficult for parents to notice when their child has become overweight than for an outside observer. As a result most children become too fat before their parents are really aware of what has happened.

Once a child has become too fat it is going to be difficult to lose that extra weight. A normal diet will keep the weight as it is and any extra food will make the child even fatter. The only way to lose weight is to give the child fewer calories than are needed. The fact that an overweight child can eat a normal or even a slightly reduced amount of food and still stay fat is a puzzle to many parents so they look for all sorts of possible reasons:

- **'it must be the glands'**
- **'it runs in the family'**
- **'her body needs to be fat'**
- **'he is happier being fat'**
- **'she gets irritable if she is thinner'**
- **'he has always been that way'**
- **'it is only a passing phase'**
- **'being fat suits her'**

One of the most important ways of checking good health and normal development for the first few months after birth is to measure the amount of weight that the baby has put on and we naturally come to see putting on weight as a good thing. There is only one way of putting on weight and that is by taking in more food energy than is necessary to stay the same size. This means that children can only become too fat by being given more food than they need for ordinary growth and development. This energy in food and drink is measured in calories and so we have:

Too Many Calories = Too Fat and Too Flabby

There is no other way of becoming overweight apart from eating or drinking too many calories. Certainly some children seem to put on weight much more easily than others and a very few have medical reasons for this, but in the end it is only possible to become fat by taking in too many calories.

Too Fat – Why Worry?

What is wrong with being a roly poly child full of jokes and smiles and seemingly without a care in the world? Why make a happy child miserable by nagging about the weight and making the child go on one diet after another? Is it really worth all the hassle and effort just to have a slimmer child? Are there really any risks to being overweight? The answers to these questions are more complicated than you might expect.

Under the age of about 5 years it seems that being overweight has much less significance than in older children. Most fat toddlers lose their excess weight and don't grow up into fat adults. However, fat school-age children are likely to remain fat into adulthood. It is not only the age of the child that is important, but it is also the amount of extra weight that makes all the difference to the risks of being overweight. Those who are slightly overweight usually have nothing like the problems that much fatter children have. Most of the research into obesity has been done in adults, but it is known that older children who are fat will tend to become fat adults and as a result have an increased risk of a wide range of problems, such as:

- **heart disease**
- **arthritis**
- **high blood pressure**
- **indigestion**
- **gall bladder trouble**
- **diabetes**
- **skin problems**
- **accidents**
- **chest problems**
- **being teased**

With such a long list of problems it's not really surprising that obese adults have a shorter life expectancy than average. So the problems are potentially serious, but there are still a lot of fat children around. Why is this? One of the reasons is that overeating quickly becomes a habit. It is then stuck as a way of life, rather like other habits such as nail biting, swearing, smoking, or driving too fast. None of these is easy to stop and, just as with eating too much, nagging people about it usually makes the habit worse.

How Fat is Too Fat?

Although fat babies are not particularly likely to grow up into obese adults, eating habits are established early on in childhood, and it is much easier to adjust food intake when children are still young than it is to cut back and to be on a slimming diet later on. When children are young, the parents have complete control over how much extra food is provided. If too few calories are given, any child will inevitably lose weight. But before you start reducing the amount of food you give you must decide if your child *is* overweight. To be quite sure you will need to take into account the following points:

- age
- sex
- height
- bone structure

There are special weight charts that tell you what percentage of children are heavier or lighter than your own child and they are easily available from most Health Centres. Height and weight checks are also done in the routine health screening tests for children. As a rule of thumb a child is overweight if the actual weight is more than 20 per cent over the expected weight for the height.

You might find it easier to judge just by looking at your child and by asking what your friends think.

Too Fat at School

Most of the complications of being too fat come later on in

adult life so the problems of obesity may not seem very relevant to children. However, fat children are likely to suffer from social and personal problems such as:

- **being called names**
- **bullying or being bullied**
- **having few friends**
- **being less good at sport (apart from swimming)**
- **finding personal hygiene more difficult**
- **having clothes not fitting**
- **feeling less good than others**

Of course some children use their obesity to their advantage by being funny and using their fatness to draw attention to themselves. This may help them feel better and cope with the social problems, but it does not reduce the long-term physical risks of being too fat.

As children develop they gradually find out what sort of person they are. In other words they develop a self image. By 8 years old the self image has become fairly stable and fixed. At this age or later, overweight children will come to see themselves as fat and possibly as somebody who is teased and joked about. The danger is that this can easily become a self-perpetuating cycle that is kept going with thoughts like:

- **'I am a fat person and I eat a lot'.**
- **'People don't like fat children'**
- **'Fat people are bad at sport'**
- **'I am not nice to look at'**
- **'I am a freak'**

School can become a very unhappy place for fat children. Some children have a special knack of searching out people's weak spots and using this knowledge for teasing or bullying. Another problem is that before puberty, fat children are often tall for their age. Being tall can cause difficulties for young children because they are mistakenly thought to be older than they are and therefore are expected to be just as clever and as well behaved as older children.

Getting the Weight Off

One of the good things about helping children to slim down before puberty is that unlike adults, all a child has to do is to stay the same weight until the increase in height catches up and balances with the weight. However, even staying the same weight can mean cutting down a lot on food if your child is very overweight. Before starting any diet it is important to be quite sure that you really do want to help your child to become slimmer. You will need all your determination and lots of motivation.

Before you do anything at all try and remember that it is no good feeling guilty about your child being overweight. It won't do you any good at all. So why not make yourself feel successful as a parent by helping your child to get some weight off? First some questions:

- **Where did the food come from that made your child fat?**
- **Who paid for it?**
- **Who prepared it?**
- **Who gave it to your child?**

Sometimes the answer will be that your child is spending lots of money on buying snacks. If this is the case, you should ask, 'Where did the money come from?' It isn't difficult to realize that parents have an important responsibility to control the food intake for their child to prevent the weight going out of control. Unfortunately most children don't know when they have had enough to eat until they have had more than they need.

Taking complete control of what your child eats may seem a bit extreme, but it is the only way that you can be sure of helping your child. It is no good leaving it to children to decide if they want to diet or not. They can't be expected to get it right.

Exercise is Good For You

Exercise is a good way of getting the extra weight off, but a lot of hard work has to go into using up those extra calories stored around the body as fat. Jogging for a quarter of an hour may not use up as many calories as there are in a bag of crisps or a can of fizzy pop. One general problem for fat children is that as they grow fatter they become less energetic, move more slowly, and therefore use up fewer calories. Here are some approximate equivalents of food and exercise:

1 pint of milk	= cycling for one hour
3 digestive biscuits	= dancing for one hour
1 serving of muesli	= one game of football
1 can of blackberries in syrup	= 3 hours watching TV!

Overweight children will usually need a great deal of encouragement to increase their activity and to exercise and you can see that a lot of exercise may be necessary to use up the calories from everyday food. It may help to go through the day and work out at each stage how your child could be involved in more exercise. For example:

- **avoiding the use of the car whenever possible**
- **walking or cycling instead of going by bus**
- **extra outdoor activities at the weekends**
- **joining a sports club**
- **being more active around the house**
- **taking a dog for a regular walk**

TAKING THE DOG FOR A REGULAR WALK....

You will need to be very clever in the way you get your child to do extra exercise because the level of motivation for this can be expected to be low. Only the most motivated children are going to be able to keep on exercising on their own, so it may well be necessary for you to organize the activity . . . and to join in yourself! Swimming, walking and cycling are the best forms of regular exercise, hopefully you may already enjoy one of these activities!

Getting High On Fibre

All plant material contains fibre which remains undigested in the bowel when cereals, fruit, or vegetables are eaten. Animal products and many refined foods do not contain fibre and so there is very little residue remaining after digestion. Although there may be slight differences in the fibre content among various plants the beneficial effect is much the same. There is some evidence that high fibre diets can reduce the frequency of several diseases of the bowel and cardiovascular system, but for slimming there are three main benefits:

- **Slowing down chewing and swallowing.**
- **Making the stomach feel full.**
- **Helping the bowel to work well.**

Those on a weight-reducing diet will find it easier if they take extra fibre – in fact it may be enough to just increase the fibre content of meals for a reduced food intake to occur. It is possible to buy specially prepared foods with high fibre, but it is often better to work out your own high fibre diet rather than just buying bran or some other specially processed food. Here are some examples of high-fibre foods that you can use:

- **vegetables**
- **fruit**
- **beans/peas/lentils**
- **most breakfast cereals**
- **bread – wholemeal/brown/ryebread**
- **dried fruit (high-calorie; use in moderation)**

It shouldn't be too difficult to make some very nice meals with these high fibre foods – baked beans on wholemeal toast, followed by some fruit would be perfect! However, if your child is fussy and refuses to eat any of these foods then at least the slimming process will be quicker . . . unless of course you give in and provide an alternative, which would in turn undo your efforts.

Which Diet?

There are so many special diets and treatments to help with slimming that it is difficult to decide which is the best. However, the idea that it is possible to eat an ordinary amount of food and calories and still lose weight is a case of muddled thinking. The truth is that weight is only lost if fewer calories are taken in than are needed. In other words, the body must be partly starved: there is no other way.

All diets work in the same way – providing less energy than is needed so that the body can burn up the extra energy that has been stored away as fat. Very low calorie diets (less than 1000 calories) can be dangerous after two or three weeks because if there isn't enough immediate energy available to the body then it will start to break down muscle protein.

Diets that are extreme or use unusual and unbalanced combinations of foods can be dangerous for children, because essential nutrients may be missing. Unbalanced diets will need to be supplemented with vitamins and minerals. Obviously you need to be particularly careful with children's diets at each stage of development. Of the more normal and balanced commercial diets there is no evidence that one is much better than any of the others, in spite of the claims that are made for each new diet as it comes onto the market. Always ask for professional advice if you are in any doubt.

Before Starting A Slimming Diet

It is easy to be put off starting a slimming diet because it can be such a lot of extra work and inconvenience. It isn't surprising that people turn to pills for an easy way out. There are several different types of tablets on the market that work in various ways, such as:

- **bulking agents to make you feel full**
- **mild laxatives to empty the bowel**
- **diuretics to get rid of fluid**
- **drugs to work on the brain**
- **drugs that increase metabolism**
- **patent remedies that do nothing much at all**

None of these tablet treatments has been shown to be

successful in the long run and none of them actually changes eating attitudes or habits. Some of the slimming pills are potentially dangerous and it is reasonable to conclude that the answer to losing weight doesn't lie in a bottle of tablets.

Whichever slimming method you decide to use there are some general principles that are helpful to follow:

- **Set a target weight that is reasonable and not too difficult to reach.**
- **All food contains calories, but *Cucumber, Celery, Carrots, Chicory, Corn, Cauliflower* and *Cabbage* are especially low so children can have as much as they can eat of these (but avoid raw cabbage stalks as they contain an anti-thyroid substance). Other vegetables and fruits are OK too.**
- **Fat has a very high content of calories for the same weight when compared with carbohydrates and proteins. Reduce fat as much as possible.**
- **High fibre foods will help to give bulk without too many calories.**
- **Slimming clubs can be very helpful in keeping you motivated.**
- **Try and keep the diet as balanced as possible.**
- **Reward charts can be very helpful. Every pound of weight lost is recorded on the chart and eventually leads to some reward.**
- **If in doubt consult your doctor or a dietitian.**

Excuses, Excuses

Getting your child to lose weight is one of the most difficult things that you can do. Not only does your child have to go against the very strong instinct of hunger, but you have to give a diet that contains fewer calories than your child actually needs. This is a mild form of starvation, which obviously means that you have to go against your own caring instinct. Because eating less than is needed for everyday living is so unnatural, most parents look for excuses to delay giving the diet properly or to stop before there has been much success.

Here are some excuses that children and parents use to avoid dieting:

- 'He is nicer when he is fat'
- 'She won't stick to a diet'
- 'It runs in the family'
- 'It is impossible to do'
- 'She will grow out of it'
- 'It is his glands you know'
- 'It is only "puppy fat"'
- 'She refuses to go on a diet'
- 'I like him fat and cuddly anyway'
- 'I have too many other things to do'

Each one of these reasons sounds quite sensible and most parents will have said something like it at one time or another. We all use excuses to get out of doing difficult things, but we shouldn't forget what the consequences might be of doing nothing or giving up. Quite apart from the consequences to the child, the chances are that doing nothing will also make the parents feel bad.

The 'Better By Half' Way of Losing Weight

The 'Better By Half' diet is a very easy and uncomplicated way to help children (aged 11 onwards) to lose weight. Younger children are growing so quickly that it should be possible to help them slim down by using less drastic methods and just keeping the weight steady as they grow, until the height and weight are balanced with each other.

I have developed the 'Better By Half' diet by combining together a number of ideas about eating problems. It is guaranteed to work if you follow it exactly as it is here!

There are three parts to the 'Better By Half' slimming method:

1. HALVE EVERYTHING

- **Give half size portions of food**
- **On a half size plate**
- **Use half size knife, fork, and spoon**
- **Eat half as quickly (twice as slowly)**
- **Half everything again (¼ quantities) if no weight is lost after a week**

2. IT'S GOOD TO BE HUNGRY

- **Hunger means that weight is being lost**
- **If your child says 'I'm hungry' you should be pleased – not worried**
- **Everytime your child feels hungry give him or her a hug or a kiss for doing so well**
- **Don't take hunger as a sign that your child needs more food, all it means is that the weight reduction is going well**

3. IT'S *YOUR* FOOD

- **Remember that you buy, prepare, and serve out most of your child's food**
- **It should be possible for you to control all of your child's food intake**
- **You may need to control your child's money if it is spent on food**
- **Don't let friends or relatives undermine your efforts by giving food**

You can see that the three parts of the 'Better By Half' approach are all quite tough on both you and your child, but it also has three advantages:

- it's uncomplicated – no calorie counting
- perception of food is different – attitudes are changed
- any cheating will be obvious – results come quickly

If the three simple principles are followed, there should be a steady reduction in weight. Any weight loss is acceptable, but about 1 lb or ½ kg per week is reasonable to aim for: remember to set an easy target weight before you start – you don't want your child to lose too much weight.

In addition to this simple approach to losing weight there are a few ideas to back up all the hard work you are doing to make sure that there is a successful outcome:

- **Check the weight once a week, on the same scales, at the same time of day, wearing the same type of clothing.**
- **If there is no weight loss in spite of keeping to the 3 rules then there must be some cheating going on somewhere – you may need to lock the larder and supervise all pocket money.**
- **Low calorie, high fibre foods are a bonus, but not really necessary for the 'Better By Half' method to work.**
- **Special dietary preparations may dangerously alter the balance of the diet and should be avoided when using the 'BBH' approach. You will save money that way, too.**
- **Reduce all snacks between meals by half or cut them out completely.**
- **Give normal amounts of milk and as much water or low calorie drinks as desired. Avoid ordinary fizzy**

and fruit flavoured drinks.

- **School meals and other meals away from home may undermine your efforts. It is best to find some way of dealing with this rather than leaving it so that the loss of weight becomes very slow.**
- **In an 'emergency', if your child is really suffering from hunger, you can offer any of the following raw vegetables – The 7 Cs: carrots, cucumber, celery, chicory, cauliflower, cabbage, corn.**

The 'Better By Half' method assumes that your child is obese (as defined on page 48) and having a normal balanced diet, in which case no adjustments to the diet should be necessary. Dangers may arise if you are giving specially prepared or unusual foods – for example, skimmed milk is low in vitamin A, soya milk is low in calcium and vitamins, and vegan diets are often low in essential nutrients. If you are in any doubt at all it is best to consult your doctor or a dietitian.

Conclusions

Children who are obviously overweight are at risk for physical, psychological, and social problems. In spite of this, the problems tend to come on slowly and may not be very obvious until it is too late. Fat children have a tough time from many different points of view and it is parents' responsibility to take control of all the food that their overweight child eats. It is no good waiting until your child is motivated to lose weight – it may be too late then.

CHAPTER 4

TOO THIN

Too Thin To Be Healthy

Some children are remarkably skinny even though they seem to eat a great deal. But how can you tell if a child is too thin? Certainly there is no harm in being a bit on the thin side. It may even be more healthy to be thinner than the weight charts show the average to be. The usual measure that is taken to be significantly too thin is where the weight is 20 per cent less than what would be expected for the child's height. Children who are underweight by this amount may well develop problems. Children who are significantly undernourished have some typical features that go together:

- **poor appetite**
- **slow healing of cuts and grazes**
- **cold hands and feet**
- **fine body hair**
- **increased activity, but easily tired**

The body is very good at adjusting to not having enough calories – after about 2-4 weeks without enough food the appetite automatically adapts and becomes less. This may be helpful for anyone ship-wrecked on a desert island with very little to eat, but for a child who is already underweight it can be an awful nuisance and make it very difficult to encourage an increased intake of food. All you will get is the response, 'I'm not hungry and I don't want to eat it'. There is also some evidence that if the food intake is insufficient for several weeks then the stomach really does become contracted so that normal amounts of food cause a feeling of being bloated, distended, and uncomfortable. The only way to overcome this is for the child to eat more and to put up with the uncomfortable feelings, knowing that he or she will get better eventually.

Poor blood circulation to the skin will not only delay healing but will also reduce the skin temperature and make the skin look pale or even blue. The development of fine body hair (called lanugo hair) occurs with more serious loss of weight. The hair has a structure that is similar to the hair of tiny babies which is gradually replaced over the first few years of life by coarser adult type hair. Why the lanugo hair develops with severe weight loss isn't known, but perhaps the reduced circulation of blood in the skin is a factor. Another skin problem is that it tends to become dry and cracks easily, causing sores to develop.

An interesting 'side effect' of losing weight is that general activity tends to increase (perhaps as a primitive protective reflex originally aimed at finding a source of food), but this activity only leads to more calories being used up. It is not difficult to see how a weight loss for whatever reason can quite quickly lead on to a vicious cycle of poor appetite, increased calorie needs, and further weight loss.

Failure to Thrive

If a baby doesn't put on weight at the expected rate there is naturally some cause for concern and this is usually called 'Failure to Thrive'. In fact it isn't that unusual for a baby not to put on weight for 2-3 weeks. Toddlers may stay the same weight for even longer and older children sometimes go several months before putting on any weight. Like most development in children the weight moves up in irregular starts and stops. If the child is ill for any reason it would be normal for the weight to go down.

There are many different illnesses that can cause failure to thrive. In most sick children the illness will be all too obvious, but sometimes it isn't at all clear what is going on – even after lots of medical tests. However, if no physical cause for the failure to thrive is found, then it could be due to psychological stress or something as simple as the child not having enough food.

Emotional stress is well known to reduce appetite and to lead to a loss of weight – although in about 10 per cent of people the result of stress is an increase in eating and in weight. Babies and young children, like everyone else, can be put off their food if they are upset. They also pick up other people's emotions very quickly – more easily perhaps than older children – and so this can also lead to eating problems.

If emotional stress is causing a poor appetite and a failure to gain weight, the reason for this is usually very obvious (although it might not be admitted to). Tension within the family for whatever reason is the most common cause for emotional stress affecting young children, but for older children school problems are also a frequent cause.

Anorexia

Anorexia means 'without appetite' and it should not be confused with anorexia nervosa which is a psychiatric disorder of eating. Loss of appetite is a very common symptom that occurs when the balance of the body and of everyday life has become disturbed for any reason. Anorexia isn't necessarily a bad sign because appetite can also be lost when children are excited or preoccupied with something interesting. However, loss of appetite in the absence of excitement or preoccupation is almost always a sign that something is wrong emotionally or physically. This makes loss of appetite a very useful sign for parents to look out for.

Loss of appetite is one of the most helpful indicators that a baby or a young child is ill – especially so because no language is needed to explain when a child has stopped eating normally. The strong connection between illness, poor appetite, and loss of weight is, of course, one of the main reasons why parents are so keen that their children should eat well, even at the risk of putting on too much weight. Perhaps it is easy to think that illness can be prevented by eating lots of food, and parents praise their children for having a good appetite and for being 'bonny'.

Poor appetite isn't the same as loss of appetite or faddiness. Children who don't feel particularly hungry are not necessarily fussy about what they eat, they just eat small amounts of food which they enjoy and then feel quite satisfied. Parents may disagree about what amount of food is too little, but the best way of deciding this is by seeing if your child is growing steadily along the correct lines for height and weight. You may need to check with your doctor about this. Even if children are rather small for their age, there is no need to worry about them so long as the height and weight are in proportion and their growth is steady.

Getting the Food Down

Here are some ideas for how you might cope with a child's poor appetite that has gone on for many months or years:

- **Gradually increase the amount of food you give your child over many months. This has to be done in such small increases that your child doesn't notice it. The increase may have to be so gradual and slow that it takes many years, so take your time and don't worry!**

- Be prepared to give extra amounts of your child's favourite food. There are usually one or two foods that a child will eat a lot of. This will help to put on weight and perhaps also increase appetite. However, it is best to give the favourite foods only after the less enjoyed food has been eaten up.
- Mix in high-calorie food supplements to your cooking. These can be bought from any chemist's shop (pharmacy). Follow the dosage instructions carefully, because supplements can be dangerous for very young children. Ask your pharmacist for details.
- Avoid making food an issue as far as possible. As soon as children realize that you are anxious about their eating, they will eat even less.
- Nagging your child to eat more will almost always make things worse.
- It might help to serve the food on a much larger plate than usual and to use a larger knife, fork and spoon to create the illusion of small amounts of food even though you have given more.
- Eating up the food quickly and having shorter meal times may also help to give the impression that

...IT MIGHT HELP TO SERVE THE FOOD ON A **MUCH LARGER PLATE**....

there isn't much food and so your child actually ends up eating more.

- If all else fails you may find that it is more effective to tell children that they can't have a particular food. 'This is special food for grown ups only – sorry you can't have any today'. Sometimes the forbidden food suddenly becomes attractive to the child who previously rejected it.
- Perhaps, after all, it would be best to accept that your child has a poor appetite and do nothing about it, provided that growth is satisfactory.

Loss of Appetite – What Does it Mean?

Loss of appetite is much more worrying than a longstanding poor appetite, because there has obviously been a change that has disturbed the normal balance of daily life. This may well be due to some form of illness, but it could also be due to emotional upset or, as is often the case, both physical illness and emotional distress acting together.

If your child is not eating as well as usual then the first thing to think about is whether it is due to physical illness. It would be very rare for any child to have loss of appetite as the only symptom of a physical or emotional illness, so there should be some other obvious signs that your child is unwell. If you are still not sure about it then check with your doctor. Signs of emotional disorder can be particularly difficult to spot and to make it even more complicated the symptoms frequently present in a physical way with tummy pains, and head and leg aches being especially frequent. Here is a list of the most common signs that a child is emotionally upset:

- Loss of appetite
- Sleep disturbance
- Irritability

- **Restlessness**
- **Poor concentration**
- **Withdrawal**
- **Worries that are excessive**
- **Crying more than usual**
- **Aches and pains**
- **Loss of interest**

Loss of appetite is just one of the symptoms of emotional disturbance, so to be sure that emotional stress is the cause of the anorexia you should expect at least two other symptoms from the check list to be present. Each of the above symptoms can occur quite normally at different stages of children's development, which is why it is important to look for a *pattern* of signs and symptoms and not just depend on one symptom alone.

A brief emotional upset that lasts only a few hours is unlikely to have much significance after a day or two, but if the disturbance goes on for several weeks it can have a major adverse effect on a child's development and future life. It is just as important to keep an eye on children's emotional state as it is to check on their physical state, and loss of appetite can be a sign of either.

In younger children who have not yet reached adolescence emotional disturbance is almost always due to something that has happened in the world outside rather than being due to inner turmoil. But as children grow older it becomes increasingly possible for the distress to be caused by a child's thoughts and inner world, although usually sparked off by some external stress. In most cases of emotional distress, it will be quite obvious what the cause is and not too difficult to put it right. However, this isn't always so – sometimes the cause of the distress is not clear at all. So to help you work out what might be going on, here are some of the less obvious reasons for children becoming emotionally disturbed:

- **Teasing or bullying.** Children often keep quiet about this because they are worried that telling parents may make things worse.
- **Failure at school.** Difficulty with reading and spelling may not be so obvious, but can cause great distress at exam times or when asked to read out loud. Failure in sports can also cause more distress than expected.
- **Loss of a friend or relative.** A brother, sister, or school friend moving away can cause much more upset than you might think. Moving house or loss of a pet can also cause problems.
- **Parental problems.** Children are quick to pick up on any problems that might affect their parent such as illness, arguments, or financial worries.
- **Relationship difficulties.** These are easy to miss because any problems are often deliberately hidden.
- **Physical, sexual, or emotional abuse.** For obvious reasons the various forms of child abuse are often kept secret.

One way of coping with strong emotions is to deny that they exist and to carry on as if nothing matters. Boys tend to do this more than girls. Sometimes the only sign that something is wrong is a loss of weight, but more often the cause of any emotional upset is all too obvious once you have actually thought of the possibility. In most cases the greater the loss of weight, the more serious is the emotional distress, but this doesn't always follow. Sometimes, of course, emotional distress can cause people to eat more than usual and put on weight.

A change of appetite is one of the most useful signs that something unusual is going on with your child, but it isn't necessarily something bad – after all a loss of appetite is one of the signs of falling in love!

Anorexia Nervosa

Loss of weight is a very common symptom and it isn't difficult to imagine that whenever your child rejects food and loses weight that it could be due to anorexia nervosa. Fortunately anorexia nervosa is quite rare (about 1 in 100,000 of the general population and 1 in 500 among 16 year olds) in spite of the large amount of attention that the media gives to it. Because it is so rare, I will only go into enough detail so that you can work out for yourself whether your child is likely to have the condition or not. The main characteristics of anorexia nervosa are as follows:

- **Marked loss of weight (more than 20 per cent of expected body weight for age and height).**
- **A feeling of being too fat.**
- **A strong wish to reduce food intake.**
- **The appetite is often not reduced, in spite of the name 'anorexia nervosa'.**
- **There is a preoccupation with food and body shape.**
- **A total lack of periods in girls even after puberty is characteristic.**
- **Overactivity and/or excessive exercise is common.**
- **The hair on the face, limbs, and back is altered to soft lanugo hair.**
- **The hormones and body chemistry become disturbed. This is mostly an effect of the loss of weight rather than the cause of it.**
- **Poor circulation leads to cold hands and feet.**
- **Cuts and grazes heal slowly.**
- **The personality is perfectionist, well behaved, and hard working.**
- **It occurs most often in older teenage girls.**
- **Loose, flowing clothes are often worn to hide the body shape.**
- **There may be an abuse of laxatives/diuretics in older cases.**

- It is rare in boys (girls/boys = 20/1). Recent evidence, however, suggests that the gap between boys and girls is closing.
- Discomfort and guilt occur on eating more than a small amount of food.
- There is often a pretence of eating more and weighing more than is the reality.

What Are the Causes?

Anorexia nervosa is a very complicated disorder of eating and there are many different factors that are thought to play a part in causing it. Social attitudes suggesting that only slim women are attractive and that fatness is unhealthy all play a part. Conversely, another theory that goes against the idea that being thin is attractive and sophisticated holds that young people with anorexia nervosa do not want to be mature and sexually attractive and so they diet to avoid this: wishing to stay looking immature and to stop the menstrual cycle. The chances are that in each individual case either theory could be true, but neither theory can explain anorexia in boys.

There is some evidence that anorexia nervosa can be picked up from other girls since it sometimes occurs in outbreaks amongst girls who know each other well. Most children don't develop anorexia nervosa until they are well into adolescence, but a few children appear to have the condition as young as 8 or 9 years of age. However, in these younger children it is much more likely that there will be some obvious form of emotional distress causing the loss of weight and many of the usual features of typical anorexia nervosa will be missing. Another possible factor is that high levels of the female sex hormone oestrogen may be a cause of nausea and loss of appetite. The sex hormones start to rise 2 years before there is any physical sign of puberty and in early adolescence the oestrogen levels are often much higher than normal.

Some cases of anorexia nervosa have experienced feeding problems early on in life and in almost every family with an anorexic child, food refusal develops into a way of communication between the child and the parent. The usual messages are as follows:

- 'I am distressed and miserable'.
- 'I worry that my feelings and my life may go out of control'.
- 'I am angry and upset'.
- 'I want you to take notice of me'.

It isn't difficult to see how food comes to be used as a method of communication because when children are young we often say things like 'You have been so good that you can have an extra sweet' or 'you have been so naughty you can't have that piece of cake'. Teenagers who develop anorexia nervosa are often particularly well behaved and doing very well in every other way. It could be that they are finding it difficult to maintain this high standard and they feel that things are going out of their control. The one thing that they can control is their food intake.

What Should You Do?

If you suspect that your child may have anorexia nervosa, it is best to seek a professional opinion at an early stage. It is easier to deal with at this stage before it has become a fixed way of life. At the same time it is also important to avoid labelling every phase when food is rejected as anorexia nervosa because this could actually fix the condition which would have otherwise faded away naturally.

Just as there are many different causes for anorexia nervosa so there are also many approaches to treatment.

There is general agreement that getting the weight back on should be given the highest priority. Helping the child to understand why it has happened comes second. There are several reasons for concentrating on weight gain first:

- **Loss of weight can itself cause loss of appetite after just a few weeks, so unless some weight is put on the appetite will remain very poor.**
- **Being very underweight produces an altered state of mind where there is an avoidance of reality. This can get in the way of treatment, but it improves as weight is put back on again.**
- **Just looking at someone who is very thin makes other people feel anxious about them which in turn will probably increase the tension over eating.**
- **Severe loss of weight can be life threatening. The most serious risk comes from a lowered resistance to infections, but if there is vomiting or excessive use of laxatives, then a loss of potassium from the body can cause serious heart problems.**

Before starting the effort of putting the weight back on again it is most important to work out what the underlying causes might be and to do what you can to sort these out. At the same time it is helpful to set a target weight that is a happy compromise between what the child wants and what the weight charts say your child's weight ought to be. A weight increase of about 1 kg per week is about the right rate to aim for, but don't worry if it is slower, so long as the weight is steadily going up. Try not to make too much of the weighing. It is best to restrict the weighing to once a week and then only under your supervision. Lock the scales away for the rest of the week!

Because weight loss and lack of adequate nutrition is potentially life threatening it is reasonable to take a very strong line about eating in this type of case. After all it could be a matter of life or death. It is no good just hoping for the best: about 5 per cent of people with anorexia nervosa die and 20 per cent continue to have longstanding problems maintaining a healthy weight. Parents often say that there is no way they can get their anorexic child to eat more, but they can't stand by and allow their children to be starved to death. Because the situation is so serious parents have to find some way or another to get the food down. This may involve taking a great deal more control over a child's eating than would usually be regarded as acceptable, such as:

- **sitting with the child until the meal is finished – no matter how long it takes – even if it takes hours.**
- **absolutely insisting that everything on the plate is finished.**
- **being prepared to be very firm indeed without losing your temper.**

These are general guidelines that you can follow, but because anorexia nervosa is such a potentially serious condition it is always best to have expert advice and support rather than struggling on alone. Once the weight has come up to somewhere near the target, it is usually the case that many of the previous problems will fade away. If they don't then any remaining underlying problems are likely to become more obvious.

- **Your determination that your child will eat MUST be stronger than your child's wish not to eat.**
- **Children's distress at having to eat everything up MUST be balanced against the possibility of death.**
- **You MUST be in control of the food because people with anorexia nervosa can't be trusted to eat properly on their own.**

Bulimia Nervosa

Bulimia is a condition of repeated vomiting that is even more rare than anorexia nervosa. The usual pattern is for the young person to eat too much – to binge, and then to feel bloated, uncomfortable, and guilty. Many of the characteristics are the same as anorexia nervosa and in about 20 per cent of cases the two conditions occur together. Bulimia is even more dangerous than anorexia nervosa for the following reasons:

- **Bulimia can occur when the weight is normal and so it is difficult to detect.**
- **Young people are so embarrassed about the vomiting that they do it very secretly and you may not know it is happening.**
- **Repeated vomiting upsets the balance of the chemicals in the body.**
- **The effect of acid on the teeth can be to destroy the dentine and cause dental caries.**
- **The most dangerous effect of repeated vomiting is a lowering of potassium in the body. A low potassium level can lead to abnormal heart rhythms without any warning.**

Repeated and deliberate vomiting is very rare in children and younger adolescents so if it does occur in that age group it is likely to be much more serious and to have a fairly obvious cause of the underlying emotional distress. The other features are very like anorexia nervosa with a similar feeling of things being out of control.

Bulimia can be helped by providing a very high level of supervision of eating in order to avoid the bingeing as far as possible. People with bulimia should be observed for at least one hour after every meal in order to stop them making themselves sick on a full stomach. This has to be done very strictly, even following the person to the toilet if

necessary. There is no point in half measures as far as
bulimia is concerned! Don't hesitate to get specialist psychiatric help for this form of eating disorder.

How to *Prevent* Anorexia
and Bulima Nervosa

Both these conditions have at their root an abnormal use of
food, a fear of the emotions and concern about food intake
going out of control. A lot can be done to help prevent the
disorders by making sure that food is never used to control
people. The use of food control can work two ways:

From parent to child.
'If you don't eat it up you won't be able to go out to
play'
'Show me that you love me and eat it up'
'If you don't eat it up I will get very upset'
From child to parent.
'I will make you cross by being fussy'
'You can't make me eat it'
'I will keep you at the table by eating slowly'

It is obviously important to try and avoid getting food and
feelings mixed up together. Mealtimes should be peaceful,
interesting, and enjoyable, rather than a time for nagging
and tension. Children are not born with an inbuilt understanding of how to control their food intake, so it is quite
reasonable for parents to have some control of eating habits,
if their child isn't managing the eating properly. To prevent
anorexia turning into a more serious state, it is important
that you are prepared to be really firm about your child
eating a reasonable amount at each meal and not holding
you and the family to ransom with threats.

   Some children are so hard to control at mealtimes. They
will try and make all the decisions about what they will and

won't eat and it is then tempting to allow them to eat separately or to make them a special meal of their own. Unfortunately if you let children take control in this way it usually makes things worse rather than better and it could even lead on to anorexia nervosa. Best to nip it in the bud and remember not to become upset yourself. Easier said than done I know, but you will have much more effect if you manage to stay cool, calm, and collected.

Conclusions

Poor appetite, loss of appetite, and food refusal occur frequently during childhood. There are many complicated reasons for each form of under-eating, so parents may have to do some detective work to find out exactly what is going on. Weight loss is more serious in childhood than later on because weight gain is normally to be expected, but at least it is a helpful sign that tells you that something has changed and the normal balance is upset. Some children use food as a way of controlling the world around them. If this is allowed to continue it can lead to more serious eating disorders.

CHAPTER 5

MAKING MEALTIMES HAPPY

The Importance of Family Meals

Sharing and eating food together is an important part of everyday life. It is a time for communication and sharing, and can be one of the few times in the day when the family gets together. In spite of this many families find that it is difficult to get everyone eating at the same table together at the same time. When children are very young it is often easier to feed them separately so that parents can eat in peace later on. When children are older they may prefer to eat on their own in front of the TV, rather than having to miss their special programme. In fact the TV has a lot to answer for! It is not at all unusual for the whole family to regularly have meals in front of the TV, rather than sitting round the table. Does this matter? Why shouldn't parents and children enjoy watching their favourite quiz game or soap opera while eating at the same time?

Why bother to have meals sitting together round a table? Isn't this a bit out of date? In many ways it is easier to get the children fed first and to keep them quiet by sitting them in front of the TV or playing a game in another room. Is there really any point in spending the extra time and energy to organize happy meals together?

Yes! It really is worth all the trouble, although it doesn't have to be like this for every meal. Here are some of the reasons why I think family meals sitting round a table are a good idea:

- **Children will learn better table manners by sitting opposite their parents and learning how to eat by copying. At the same time the parents can see how well the children are managing.**
- **Meals are a good time for family communication because everyone is together and not distracted by other things going on.**
- **It is a good time for children to learn by listening to 'grown up talk' and to join in themselves.**
- **Mealtimes are one of the few occasions when everyone in the family naturally comes together. Just being together in the same place and doing the same thing helps to reinforce the family as a unit.**
- **Children can learn to play a useful part in family life by helping to prepare the meal, lay the table, or by clearing up afterwards.**
- **By learning to sit at the table and wait for the food to arrive or for others to finish, children can be helped to develop self control.**

Of course when children are still very young it is too much to expect them to sit through a whole mealtime that may take 20 minutes or longer, but it is something to aim for by gradually increasing the time your child is expected to stay at the table.

Table Manners

There is a wide variation in what table manners are acceptable in one family and not in another. Even such minor things such as how to hold a knife may be seen as very important. Some families say 'hold it like a pencil', others say 'put the pointing finger along the blade' and yet other families say 'don't use a knife – use a fork'. In view of this variation and disagreement about table manners, it might be assumed that they don't matter too much – but they do! Whenever we meet somebody new we all tend to look for small clues to tell us something about the person. Table manners are one way that we use to assess the type of person and how they have been brought up. The conclusions that we come to are often completely wrong and based on predjudice, but we do it just the same.

Children are clearly at a disadvantage if their table manners are very different from 'normal'. However, all parents will have their own idea about what is meant by good manners and it is vital to reach some agreement about what standards to set and then to keep to them.

Of course, children are not born with naturally good manners. Throwing food about is quite normal when children first start feeding themselves and it isn't until about 5 years of age that children can manage a knife and fork reasonably well, and even then they will still need your help at times. By 8-10 years old most children will be aware of the basic rules of table manners and will be quick to notice others who have different standards – especially a brother or sister! However, some of the rules of eating may seem to have little sense to them and at moments of relaxation or great hunger children of any age will forget their manners and do what comes naturally.

Teaching Good Table Manners

Teaching table manners is best done by example, but some active teaching is also helpful. Here are some ideas about how to teach good eating habits:

- **It is important to start teaching good manners before your child eats in public without you, for example at parties or meals at school.**
- **If you are unsure about what is generally accepted, ask your friends, but don't be surprised if they disagree with each other!**

- Make sure that all the adults at home are agreed on the main rules and are setting a good example.
- Keep the teaching as brief as possible, otherwise meal times may start to feel like school lessons.
- Try and keep a sense of humour about table manners so that meals don't become tense and unpleasant.
- Rather than nagging on and on about table manners, it may help to have a 'blitz' on them every now and then. Warn your child beforehand, 'Today is good table manners day!' or 'Who would like to win a prize for having good table manners during the whole of this meal?'
- Take a long-term view and don't get upset about every little mistake that your child makes.
- If your child is able to have good manners on important occasions, you can relax and be pleased, even if everyday manners are not perfect – whose are?

The most common mistake that parents make is to expect too much and to set a standard of behaviour that is too high for their child's stage of development. There is then a danger that a battle will develop between parent and child, which the child can always win if it involves eating (by refusing food or by being sick). It is always important to distinguish between the times when your child has bad manners on purpose to get at you and when it is due to forgetfulness or laziness. Deliberately bad table manners are obviously a disciplinary matter, but in other cases all that is needed is a bit more training.

How can you teach your child good table manners without endless nagging and telling off at meal times? Here are some light hearted ways of 'teaching without tears'. None of them involves being critical or getting angry, but they make the point clearly enough:

- **Talking with the mouth full** — *'I can't understand what you are saying'*
- **Eating messily** — *'Here is a bib for you to wear'*
- **Eating too quickly** — *'You like waiting at the end of the meal?'*
- **Eating too slowly** — *'I hope you finish in time for pudding'*
- **Elbows on the table** — *Try a lower chair or elbow cushions!*
- **Holding the knife badly** — *Smaller cutlery is easier to hold*

Sitting at the Table

At what age should children be able to sit at the table for their meal? Some parents prefer to have a peaceful meal separate from their children, but it is a good idea to have them joining in as soon as possible – first of all sitting nearby in a 'baby sitter' and feeding tray and later in a high chair at the table. Your child will then be able to learn from watching you eat and will copy you without the need for too much nagging and telling off.

When children are old enough to sit on an ordinary chair they will be keen to get down as soon as they have finished their meal – if not before – and it is much easier to slide off a normal chair than a high one. It is not unusual for young children to find it very difficult to sit at the table for long periods of time. As soon as the immediate feeling of hunger has been satisfied they see no reason to stay at the table when sitting there is boring and there are so many interesting toys to play with. To remain sitting at the table requires self control.

Self control starts to develop very early on in childhood and by the time a child goes to school it is important that a reasonable level of 'inner' self control has been achieved, otherwise there are likely to be problems with concentration and learning. It may seem a big jump from sitting at the meal table to making good progress at school, but there *is* a connection: unless a child can remain in one place for more than a few minutes, it will be difficult for him to sit quietly and learn properly.

Self control can only be developed if control is given from the outside first, it doesn't just grow by itself. By insisting that your child sits at the table throughout the meal you are giving the sort of external control that is needed for any child to develop self control. One way of looking at this inner control is that it is a bit like children carrying around a clear memory of their parent inside their heads and then 'hearing' the parent say what should be done. To begin with the real parent says 'You must stay sitting at the table', then when the inner control has been established the 'parent memory' says the same thing inside the child's head – at least for some of the time! Eventually the real parent can relax and rely on this inner voice to give the necessary self control that every child needs.

The process of gaining self control is very important – without it the child will be disruptive and even dangerous. This is the real art of being a parent, because you have to strike a fine balance between being over controlling and not giving enough control and guidance. At the same time this balancing point is changing all the time as each child grows older. Parents also need to be in tune with what is happening inside their child's mind and what stage of self control he or she has managed to achieve. Don't be surprised if all this sounds rather complicated . . . it is!

Here are some guidelines for helping your child gain self control:

- **The external control that you give your child needs to be very clear and firm to begin with. This doesn't mean smacking or being unpleasant, but it may mean speaking very firmly and seriously and being prepared to physically move a young child in** order to back up what you have said.

- As your child grows older, it should be possible to give less and less external control, but get the same result.
- Children show by their behaviour how much self control they have developed so it isn't too difficult to tell what progress you are making.
- Some children need much more external control than others, so don't give up just because it is hard work or because it seems to be taking a long time. Learning how to have self control is a process that goes on and on – after all who do you know with *perfect* self control?
- The rate at which you fade out the outside control must be matched to the progress in the development of inner control.
- If you are not sure what level of self control to expect at different ages, you can check this out with your friends and see what they think. A reasonable goal to aim for is that by the time your child has started school, he or she should be able to sit in one place for 10-15 minutes or more, even if it is boring and nothing much is happening. By the time your child is a teenager the time of being able to stay in one place should have increased up to one hour or more.

If a young child at school can't sit in a chair for more than a minute or two then it is going to be difficult to teach reading and writing skills or to build up concentration. Sitting at the meal table is a natural time to help your child to learn how to remain sitting in a chair. The advantage of learning at mealtimes is that they occur regularly and often. If you are sitting round a table you will be able to deal immediately with any problem of control. Meals take about the right time for young children to be expected to sit in one place, and if they begin to feel restless there is the end of the meal to look forward to.

After all this theory, how do you actually get an active and unwilling child to sit at the table? To a large extent this is really a matter of discipline (see my book *Bad Behaviour* for more details on methods of discipline). However, there are two straightforward things that you can do:

- **Try and fix a routine for mealtimes so that sitting at the table becomes part of a habit. Children enjoy regular routines and benefit from them. Once the habit is established, sitting at the table will be just as automatic as getting up in the morning. In other words, it will be something that happens without thought or argument. Keep at it!**
- **Often the main problem is how to *keep* children sitting at the table for more than a few minutes. The most effective way of dealing with this in most cases is to have a rule that once children get down from the table, the meal is over as far as they are concerned – even if they are only halfway through the first course. But this will only work if no snacks are given between meals: your 'trump card' of hunger is once again useful and will make this approach work. However, it is important to feel confident about what you are doing and only to use it as part of a carefully worked out plan that all the adults at home agree with (see guidelines on using hunger, pages 36-39).**

'Table Talk'

Some families have strict rules about not talking at the table, but this is a shame because it means missing out on a good opportunity for children to learn a great deal. The no-talking rule probably goes back to the days when food was more scarce and meals were seen as a gift from God that

SOME FAMILIES HAVE STRICT RULES ABOUT
NOT TALKING.....

should be eaten in respectful silence.

Obviously children can learn a lot by listening to adults talking and the special advantage of doing this at the table is that the children are a captive audience. At other times of the day they are likely to be doing other things and unless what you are talking about is very interesting, they won't listen. Table talk is therefore a marvellous way of teaching your children about all sorts of things without it being obvious. Many children put up the barriers as soon as they think that they are being taught at home. Table talk can avoid this.

Children learn by example and they will undoubtedly want to join in the discussions. It won't be long before everyone is talking, with very little listening going on. There is no harm at all in being quite strict about people taking turns to talk, even if this may seem artificial. Children need to learn how to listen as well as to express themselves.

Mealtimes are a useful time to find out what everyone in the family has been doing and to generally keep in touch with each other. It is a natural time to come together, without having to make special arrangements. Parents who work long hours or shifts may find it difficult to organize meals together, and although this fact of life has to be accepted, it is worth making a lot of effort to organize family meals together as many times in the week as possible.

Helping the Family

When the family meets round the meal table and shares food together, it is a natural way of reminding everyone that as well as being individuals they are also members of the family unit. There is a need for family members to work together to support the family. Parents often find it hard to judge the level of help that children of different ages should be giving to the family. Most parents expect very little from their children, and as a result get very little. A few parents expect far too much help, even to the point of exploitation. Listen to what your child tells you, and if you are still not sure that you have got it right ask your friends.

The contribution that is reasonable varies with the age of the child, but it is a good idea to start as soon as possible so that, like sitting at the table, it becomes a habit, a normal routine of everyday life and not something to be argued about. When children can walk safely it is reasonable to ask them to carry small items to and from the table. Very young children may be able to stand on a chair and 'wash up', even if all this means is moving things around in the water. All this takes extra time, but it is certainly worth it in the long run.

Parents often complain that they have to keep nagging at their children to help. Sometimes this is such a bore that it is easier to forget the children and do it oneself. Of course, the more you do the less your child will want to do. Here are some ideas about how to get children to help with family meals:

- **Remember that most children aren't born naturally helpful, most will take the easy way out and do as little as possible.**
- **Spontaneous helpfulness is rare in children and**

most have to be taught how to be helpful.

- **Most children need to be told exactly what to do and then to be supervised to make sure that it is done.**

- **Some children are much more lazy than others. They will need a lot of extra teaching and practice in being helpful.**

- **Some parents prefer not to ask their children to help, either because it produces no result or because they feel it is wrong. Whichever way it is, the end result is that the children become more and more unhelpful.**

- **Start training your child to be helpful as early as possible so that it becomes part of the normal mealtime routine.**

- **One way of getting children to be helpful is to ask them to do whatever it is *before* the meal. The meal obviously can't be started until the job is done. (Once again you can use the hunger trump card as outlined on pages 36-7.)**

- **Another way is to make out a daily check list or chart of family chores and put it up on the kitchen wall as a reminder for everyone. Any job not done could be repeated twice by the lazy or forgetful child who obviously needs more practice in being helpful.**

Conclusions

There is more to an ordinary family meal than you might expect. Children can learn social skills and develop their ability to communicate. Not only can children increase their general knowledge by listening to adults talking at mealtimes, but they can increase their self control and ability to be helpful. The family unit itself is reinforced by shared meals together. It is amazing what can go on during a normal everyday meal!

CHAPTER 6

EATING PROBLEMS: QUESTIONS AND ANSWERS

Parents usually ask two types of questions when they have been given some advice. 'Yes but . . .' is what you are likely to say if you are not really convinced that the advice is correct and you can think of all kinds of reasons why you should not believe it. The 'What if . . .' questions are asked by parents who think the advice seems sensible, but they can see reasons why it might not work.

Yes But . . .

'I think that diet affects children's behaviour much more than you say'

In many ways it seems obvious that 'we are what we eat'. Some foods like prunes or beans, or drinks such as coffee or alcohol contain substances that if consumed in sufficient quantities will affect anybody's behaviour in one way or the other! However, the claims that food allergies cause difficult behaviour in children are probably exaggerated. Any link between food allergies and difficult behaviour may be indirect and due to having fewer allergic symptoms, rather than a direct effect on how children behave. Allergies make people feel uncomfortable and unwell so it isn't surprising that when a child's physical health improves, there is also an improvement in behaviour. There are various theoretical explanations that make scientific sense, but none of them has yet been proved beyond doubt in practice. Most research that has been carefully carried out shows that it is only a small number of children whose behaviour seems to be affected by food allergy and they are likely to be allergic in other ways as well, such as hayfever, asthma, and eczema. Many research projects are unsatisfactory because either the research observer or the parent is aware which diet the child is on, and many studies don't follow through the research, monitoring the child on the diet followed by a period off and then on again to be absolutely sure what effect the diet has.

Some foods are known to make children behave well! The promise of a sweet or some other favourite food will usually improve a child's behaviour greatly!

'My son's behaviour improved as soon as I removed artificial colourings from the diet'

That's good! But it does not *prove* that the colourings were actually causing the bad behaviour. One alternative explanation is that in the past your child didn't believe that you really meant it when you said 'No'. Perhaps your child has been impressed that you have been so clear about what can and can't be eaten and is now taking more notice of other things that you say? Another possible reason is that you are now feeling more positive about your child because you feel that there is something practical you can do to help him. The main food colourings that were known to cause allergic reactions have been removed from foods likely to be eaten by young children.

'I have heard that sugar can cause behaviour problems'

There have been reports that sugar can cause delinquency and learning problems. Research studies in America have claimed to show that reducing the sugar content of school meals and even prison meals results in improved behaviour. Unfortunately each study can be criticized, mainly on the grounds of observer bias. The link between sugar and the brain is not yet fully understood, but there has been some research that suggests that sugar may have the effect of increasing the level of endorphines in the brain tissue (morphine-like chemicals produced by the body). This would certainly help to explain why children are prepared to do all kinds of things just for a sweet.

'Hair analysis showed a deficiency in zinc so this must be why my daughter has anorexia'

There probably is a link between very low zinc levels in the body and poor appetite. However, zinc is widespread in food and low levels are extremely unlikely to occur unless there is excessive loss due to vomiting and diarrhoea. It is best not to trust hair analysis since it is a very unreliable test – just try sending two hairs from the same person for analysis at two different laboratories – it is most unlikely that the two results will be the same!

'I don't enjoy eating with the children as they behave so badly at the table. I would rather eat separately'

This is a shame, but it is not unusual for mealtimes to be disrupted until children have learnt the rules of eating at the table. You can't expect too much from young children,

" I don't enjoy eating with the children..."

but it really is worthwhile putting a lot of effort into getting your child to behave well at mealtimes, for the following reasons:

- **Mealtimes occur three times daily. It is not much fun having to look forward to bad behaviour three times daily.**
- **You will enjoy meals if your child behaves well.**
- **If you can't even get good behaviour from your child at mealtimes, you are unlikely to get it at other times.**
- **It is embarrassing to take a child out for a meal or even to see relatives if your child has bad table manners.**
- **Mealtimes are a good time for family communication and enjoyment. This will be lost if you have to spend all the time dealing with bad behaviour.**

'I don't think young children should eat with adults'

Perhaps not for the first two or three years, but the sooner children do eat with grown ups, the quicker they will learn good table manners. A good compromise is to have one meal a day when everybody eats together.

'I don't agree with forcing a child to sit at the table for meals'

There should be no need to use force. Your insistence and determination to make this part of the normal daily routine should be enough. If you only provide food for children who are sitting properly at the table, your child will soon get the message, provided that you don't give too many snacks between meals. When the meal is finished and the grown ups want to talk, there is no reason why the children shouldn't get down from the table if you can trust them to play without supervision.

'I would much prefer my child to be happy and fat than thin and miserable'

Certainly a child's mood is more important than his or her size. Unfortunately it is a myth that fat people are happier than thin ones. In fact there is a lot of evidence to show that fat children are actually distressed and unhappy underneath their happy appearance. They usually have to put up with a lot of teasing as well as having difficulty finding clothes to fit. Fat children are more likely to have accidents and in the long run being too fat leads to serious risks to health.

'Children should be allowed to eat what they like'

If children are brought up on the principle that they know best, sooner or later there are likely to be problems with other issues as well as eating. However, it is reasonable to make a note of what your child likes and take it into account when you are preparing a meal. One or two food fads are quite acceptable and not infrequently they are due to allergy to the foods in question. Try and keep it so that your child expresses an opinion and then you make the decisions.

'My children behave much better if they eat in front of the T.V.'

That is not surprising because it will keep their attention, but it won't help family communication or the learning of good table manners from you. You could think about ways of making mealtimes round a table more interesting than the TV!

'I insist that my daughter eats up all the food on her plate'

There is a danger that this will develop into a battle of wills if your child has to remain at the table after the meal has finished. It is best for everybody to end the meal at the same time and all help with clearing up together. Any uneaten food can be thrown away, given to the cat or made into soup. If your daughter realizes that she can use 'not eating' to wind you up, she is likely to continue to do so.

'There is no way I can stay calm while my son refuses to eat'

It would be surprising if you could stay calm because it is such a difficult thing to do. But part of being a parent is learning how to keep your own upset feelings away from children – except on those occasions when it could be helpful for your child to know what you are feeling. A mealtime is one of those occasions when it is no good getting upset and showing your feelings, it only makes things worse. Plan in advance what you will do if your child refuses to eat something so that your emotions don't get the better of you. Keep practising at pretending to be unconcerned about your son's food refusal (see Chapter 4 Too Thin).

'I can see no harm in giving snacks during the day and sweets after school'

A snack between meals may be very necessary for young children who need to have a good supply of energy and may become irritable if hungry. But as children grow older there is a risk that snacks will put children off their food at mealtimes. The problem with regularly giving sweets after school and ice cream whenever the van comes round is that children can easily become very demanding and difficult, and they come to expect sweets as a right and get upset if they can't have their own way. In the end all you are left with is an annoyed child with a poor appetite.

'My whole family has been fat for generations and they have had no problems'

It isn't unusual for fat children to come from overweight families. It could well be that there are genetic factors that make your family use food very efficiently and therefore need fewer calories than most people. In other words only small amounts of food are needed to keep the weight steady. However, there is only one way of getting fat and that is to eat and drink more calories than are necessary.

There is good evidence that being overweight is dangerous to health in many different ways. Being fat is probably more dangerous to men than women and especially so if the weight is put on around the abdomen. The fact that Great Uncle Tom lived to a ripe old age in spite of being fat doesn't make the risks for anyone else in the family any less. Some families eat two or three times as much as they need to and in this case it may be impossible to get a child to lose weight unless the whole family changes the way they eat.

'How do I know if my child is getting the right sort of food?'

If your child eats a wide range of food with plenty of fresh fruit and vegetables, you can't go far wrong. Try and avoid food that has been processed (manufactured) because this tends to destroy the nutrients. Too much of any one type of food is also unhealthy. Fresh natural foods are the best. The body is amazingly good at getting the best out of even very poor food.

'What If . . .'

'My child has to have a special diet for medical reasons'

There are many medical disorders where a special diet is needed. Diabetes is a common reason, but there are many others where eating normal foods can have very serious results. Parents have to be extremely determined if they want to keep their children on a strict diet. It may help to see the diet as rather like a medicine that has to be taken even though it isn't very nice. Parents always find some way of getting the medicine down and the child soon realizes that there is little point in resisting the parents' total determination.

'My fat son refuses to go on a diet to lose weight'

You don't need to worry too much about special diets even though there are lots of them available commercially. You don't even have to bother about counting calories. All that is needed is to give less food to your son until he eventually loses some weight and then keep him on that amount which will probably be enough to keep the weight steady at the correct level. There is no need to tell him that he is on a diet, after all it is your food that you have bought and prepared. As a parent it is your responsibility to make decisions about what is right for your child and remember that you control his food.

Another approach is to give your child food that is high in fibre and low in calories. This will make the amount of food look the same without being fattening. Unfortunately, low-calorie, high-fibre foods are often the foods that most children dislike!

Increasing exercise is another way of helping children to lose weight. Obvious things such as swimming and cycling are helpful, but so is an increase in everyday activity around the house. You could ask your son to help you with the cleaning and to fetch and carry things for you.

'I have done everything I can to help my daughter lose weight, but I don't think that I am strong enough to resist her demands for food'

The trouble with food is that it is so important in the early relationship between parent and child. Food continues to be symbolic of parental love, and stopping a child from eating is like saying 'I don't love you'. However, one very important form of parental love is to say 'no' as a way of caring and keeping the child safe.

If all else fails, it may be possible for a relative to help out. Your daughter could go away during the school holidays to stay with somebody who is prepared to help her lose weight and whom you can trust to be firm about it. This can work very well, but it is vital to avoid the weight going back on again when she returns home.

'My daughter managed to lose weight, but then put it on again even though she was not eating any more than before'

Fat children usually move less quickly and play less sport than children of normal weight. This can mean that fat children require fewer calories to maintain a steady weight than thinner children. However, when fat children lose weight they then need even fewer calories. This is due to something called thermogenesis where the body tissues (lean body mass) use up energy just to keep the cells ticking over and obviously fat people usually have more cells to keep going.

'I have put my fat son on a diet and he has been very good in keeping to it, but he has lost no weight'

Either your diet is not strict enough or your child is cheating and eating more than you realize. You had better check where the loopholes are:

- **Is your child having school lunches? If he does let the school know about the diet and ask for smaller portions to be served. Then keep checking that this is in fact happening.**
- **Are friends or relatives giving your child extra food?**

- **Is the pocket money being spent on food? It may help for your child to keep an account book so that you can see where the money is going. You may even have to take control of all the money and only allow it to be spent under your supervision.**
- **Is your child taking food without asking (stealing)? You may have to count biscuits, sweets, and anything else that can be easily taken. You may even have to lock the food away.**
- **Could your child be getting extra calories from drinks? Most drinks have a high calorie content. Don't forget that milk is a food.**
- **Is your child getting enough exercise?**

'My daughter screams if she can't get down from the table as soon as she has finished'

If you let her get down from the table every time she screams she will always use this method for communication because it works so well. It is a good idea to have a family rule about getting down from the table and to stick to it. It is probably best to get your child to wait until everyone has finished. This will teach her to develop self control and saves you from getting indigestion as she rushes around.

'I can't get my son to eat anything new and unfamiliar'

This is a common problem. Children generally like to keep to the familiar foods and eating habits – it makes them feel secure. Don't be put off if your son rejects a new food, just try again later, at another meal. Take it slowly and use hunger to motivate eating. This means introducing new foods when you know that your son is really hungry. As soon as you have got him eating a reasonably balanced diet, you can relax and take your time over any further introductions of new foods.

'I am convinced that my daughter is allergic to milk products'

Intolerance to cows' milk and milk products is quite common, especially in young children. Fortunately most children grow out of this as they get older. So even if your child is sensitive to milk it is worthwhile trying the milk again from time to time. The same applies to other food allergies as well.

'My daughter is sick if I make her eat cabbage or fish'

If there is no evidence of food allergy (no other allergies, no rash, tummy ache, or diarrhoea) then it may help to see this as a food phobia. Some children certainly behave as if they have an extreme fear of certain foods. Food 'phobias' are best dealt with by giving very small amounts of the feared food until it can be tolerated in larger amounts.

'My son only eats crisps, sausages, bread and bananas'

Even on a very restricted diet most children develop satisfactorily. It is interesting that many faddy children seem to be quite bright and do particularly well at school, but there is often a stubborn side to their personality. Because of this stubbornness, very faddy children are usually difficult to change. Once you have checked that your child is medically fit and growing well, you have three options:

● **Do nothing**. Your son will continue to grow and do

well, but eating out with friends may be a problem.
His personality is likely to remain rather rigid and
stubborn.

- *Go all out to stop the food fads*. This will be hard
going and probably full of drama. You just insist
that he eats what you give him and nothing else. If
you are very determined and use the hunger drive,
there is no reason why you shouldn't win through
in the end.

- *Compromise*. Each time you sit down to a family
meal, give your child everything that is being
served, but only small portions of the food you
know he doesn't like. Expect this to be eaten and
follow the guidelines given on page 39.

'My son has invited a friend with food fads for a meal at home'

It is worthwhile fitting in with known food fads of friends
– within reason. It isn't worth getting upset if your food is
refused and there is no point at all trying to get the friend
to change the habits of a lifetime. However, it is best not to
cook the friend anything separate from your child as this
will actually encourage fussiness.

'I give up!'

It isn't at all unusual for parents to feel quite desperate
because their children won't eat properly or because they
are either too fat, too greedy, too fussy, or too thin. The
problem occurs at every mealtime, but don't give up. Look
at all the things that your child can do well, even if one of
these is to be very stubborn and self willed! Stubborn
children often do very well in life because they have the
determination that is necessary for success.

It is important to remember that you are a good parent in

many ways and that you can be successful. For this reason it is often helpful to focus on just one small area of eating behaviour at a time and then keep at it until you have got it right. Start with something fairly easy before going on to tackle the main problems.

If you really feel that you are getting nowhere, there is no harm in giving up for a few days or weeks. We all need a rest from time to time.

I have done everything you have suggested, but my child still has serious eating problems. I think I need professional help for my child.

Here are some suggestions if you feel it is necessary to get some outside help:

- **Ask other parents and professionals what they know of the local services, but take what they say with a pinch of salt, because individual opinions may be unreliable. One of the best informed people is likely to be your G.P.**
- **Voluntary groups for parents can be very supportive and give you an idea of how other people have coped. But they don't give professional advice, although they should be able to advise on how to get this type of help.**
- **There is a wide range of professional groups who have specialized training and experience with children's emotional and behavioural problems. The difference between the various professions is confusing to say the last. One way round this problem is to ask your G.P. to refer you to the local Child Psychiatry Service where it is usual for a range of different professionals to work closely together.**

APPENDIX

WHAT THE RESEARCH SHOWS

Eating is a vital part of everyday life, so it is not surprising that any difficulties with feeding can cause very strong emotions. And vice versa: strong feelings can result in eating problems. This close relationship between food and feelings is the cause of considerable concern for parents. Most of the worry about children's eating is unnecessary, because the majority of childhood eating problems resolve spontaneously. But at the same time most of the eating problems of adult life can be traced back to childhood (Brandon 1970), so it is important for parents to have a good understanding of what the issues are.

Surveys

Parents of preschool children express more concern about feeding and sleeping problems than anything else. The National Child Development Study followed up all children born during the week 5-11 April 1970 and found that 13 per cent had feeding problems as a baby and about 40 per cent of those also had sleeping difficulties (Butler and Golding 1986). The same survey found that feeding problems in very young children were likely to be associated with the following factors:

- **Moving home**
- **Having a young mother**
- **Being an only child**
- **Having a low birth weight**

By the time that the children started at school these asso-
ciations were no longer significant. However, 24 per cent of
5 year olds were described as being faddy and these were
likely to come from smaller and better off families. Only
one per cent were thought to be overeating. Children with
feeding problems were more likely to have stomach aches,
vomiting, and headaches, but there is no way of telling if
this was due to a common factor such as food allergy.

An important survey of 11-year-old children living on the
Isle of Wight was carried out by the 'father' of child psychiatry in the UK, Professor Michael Rutter and his colleagues. They found that the rate of eating problems of all
kinds was about 20 per cent as reported by parents (Rutter
et al 1970). And like other similar surveys there was no
difference between boys and girls in the rate of eating
difficulties.

Obesity

Childhood obesity appears to be increasing in frequency in
western countries. In the USA it seems to be reaching
epidemic proportions, where about 10 per cent of preschool children are overweight (Maloney and Klykylo
1983). In the UK another National Survey – where all children born between 3 and 9 May 1946 were carefully
followed into adulthood – found that 16 per cent were
overweight for height and the same number were underweight (Crisp *et al* 1970). The follow-up of these children
into adult life showed that there was a strong tendency for
the obesity to continue. In another longterm follow-up
study of children into adult life it was reported that 36 per

cent of infants whose weight exceeded the 90th percentile (ie. heavier than 90 per cent of children at that age) were reported to become obese adults (Charney *et al* 1978). Even more striking is the finding that at least 80 per cent of fat five year olds become fat adults (Bayrd 1978). It does seem that an onset of obesity after the age of 4 years has a much worse prognosis than an onset in infancy (Shapiro *et al*, 1984). One possible explanation for this is that adipose cells only multiply under the influence of prolonged and marked obesity (Poskitt 1980). Childhood obesity therefore has more significance in school-age children than in infancy. A review of treatment for obesity by Susan Spence (1986) suggests that attitudes and fixed behaviour patterns need to be the focus of the dietary effort rather than just giving a diet and hoping for the best.

The Causes of Eating Problems

Various family factors such as parental attitude to food, fatness, family diet and eating habits have been implicated. In a study of eating problems in 11-year-olds Professor Sidney Brandon found that the difficulties with eating were associated with the following factors:

● **Problems in the parent–child relationship**
● **Emotional stress in the mothers**
● **Difficulties in the marriage**

It is not easy to tell if these problems were the result or the cause of having a child who is difficult about eating (Brandon 1970). A multitude of causes for obesity have been postulated and there is evidence for both genetic and environmental causes. The family factors that lead to a tendency to be obese have been reviewed by Lorna Hecker and her colleagues (1986). They suggested that emotional conflicts and psychological factors have been identified as important in causing obesity. Fat children are more frequently reported to be:

- **overdependent on their mothers**
- **often inactive**
- **more likely to be an only child or youngest child**
- **easily comforted by food**
- **more likely to have abnormal body image**

The genetic influence on obesity was investigated in a Danish study of 540 children adopted at birth. It was found that in adults there was a significant link between the overweight adopted adults and their overweight siblings from whom they had been separated at birth and had been brought up in a different environment (Sorensen *et al* 1989). The evidence for a genetic factor in producing obesity seems therefore to be very strong, but it is important to remember that the only way to get fat is to eat more food than is necessary. In other words, where there is a genetic predisposition to obesity then a smaller amount of food than normal will be required to maintain a steady weight.

Food and the Brain

A detailed review of the effects of diet on brain function by Steven Zeisel (1986) notes that the brain requires a large amount of energy in the form of glucose in order to function properly. In fact the brain uses about two thirds of the sugar available in the body. Undernutrition in the weeks just before and after birth can have an adverse effect on brain function which may be lasting and result in poor school performance and an increased rate of behaviour problems. Going without breakfast in the morning seems to cause children with learning problems to do even worse in school tasks, but has little or no effect on bright children.

It has been claimed that sugar causes difficult and aggressive behaviour in school children and that it interferes with learning. There may be some evidence that sugar may increase movement in children, but there is no convincing evidence that sugar affects other aspects of behaviour. Caffeine in coffee and tea does not increase brain power although it does have a general alerting effect. Caffeine has no effect on children's behaviour.

Food Allergy

Food allergies are quite common in young children during the first few years of life, but become less frequent as they grow older so that by the age of five years most of the problems have resolved. The chief symptoms are diarrhoea, abdominal pain, and skin rashes. Cows' milk, eggs, wheat, fish, pork, and beef have been implicated in allergic colitis and there have been suggestions that it may progress into Crohn's disease – a potentially serious inflammation of the bowel in older people (Hill and Milla 1990). The link between food allergy and food fads has not been well researched. Certainly children will eventually learn to avoid any food that produces severe symptoms, but if the reaction is mild or delayed the child may not make the connection and will continue to eat the food without realizing the trouble that it is causing. This makes it rather unlikely that food fads are in fact unrecognized food allergies.

Hyperactivity and Diet

There is controversy about what constitutes hyperactivity in children. The following points are some of the issues that make hyperactivity so complicated:

● **Young children are naturally active as a normal**

part of development
- **The difference between normal and abnormal activity is difficult to define**
- **Children's behaviour is very variable and easily affected by changes in the environment**
- **Parents vary in how much hyperactivity they can cope with and not unusually believe that their child is hyperactive when in fact the behaviour is quite normal for a child of that age**
- **Hyperactivity is sometimes called attention deficit disorder or the hyperkinetic syndrome and sometimes hyperactivity is used as a word to describe generally difficult and disobedient behaviour – all this confusion makes the term almost meaningless**
- **Hyperactivity should be associated with a short attention span, being distracted easily and impulsiveness for a proper diagnosis to be made**
- **The diagnosis of hyperactivity needs to be made by a child specialist**

There are theoretical reasons why salicylates that occur naturally in food might have an effect on behaviour through their influence on the production of prostaglandins in the brain. Feingold and his colleagues in America claimed to be able to show that removing salicylates as well as artificial colourings and preservatives from the food of hyperactive children resulted in an improvement within a few days in at least 50 per cent of cases.

Unfortunately, these early investigations were not carried out in a scientific way, and it is likely that the improvement was due to the 'halo' effect of a special diet. Properly controlled research suggests that only a very small number of children are affected by food additives and an even smaller number improve on an exclusion diet (some estimates suggest 25 per 100,000 children). One of the better controlled studies was carried out by Dr Egger and his colleagues at Great Ormond Street Children's Hospital

(Egger *et al*, 1985). This research is often quoted as proof that food allergy affects behaviour, but even in this study there are problems in that the children were a highly allergic group and some of the findings were difficult to explain.

A more recent study carried out at the Brompton Hospital for Chest Diseases in London (Pollock and Warner 1990) investigated 19 children whose parents thought that their behaviour was affected by food additives. The children were given an exclusion diet together with either placebo pills or active pills that contained large amounts of the four food additives that are most frequently claimed to cause behaviour problems. The children were rated as slightly more difficult when taking the additives, but not enough for most of the parents to notice, in spite of their claims. The effects of additives were seen within 12 hours and did not continue for more than a day or so. Although 40 per cent had evidence of some form of allergy there was no connection between allergic symptoms and rates of behaviour problems.

The conclusion that can be drawn from the research is that food additives and some foods can affect behaviour either by some form of dose dependent intoxication as with caffeine or alcohol, or by intolerance as with food additives, possibly mediated by allergic mechanisms affecting histamine or prostaglandins.

REFERENCES

Bayrd, E, *The Thin Game*. New York, Newsweek Books (1978).

Brandon, S, An epidemiological study of eating disturbances, (1970). *J. Psychosom. Med.* 14, 253-257.

Charney, E., Chamblee, H., McBride, M. *et al*, The childhood antecedents of adult obesity: do chubby infants become obese adults? (1976). *New Engl. Med.*, 195:6-9.

Crisp, A.H., Douglas, J.W.B., Ross, J.M., Stonehill, E, Some developmental aspects of disorders of weight, (1970). *J. Psychosom. Med.* 14, 327-345.

Egger, J., Carter, C.M., Graham, P.J., Gumley, D., Southill, J.F., Controlled trial of oligoantigenic treatment in the hyperkinetic syndrome, (1985). *Lancet*, i:540-545.

Feingold, B.F, *Why Your Child Is Hyperactive*, New York, Random House (1974).

Hecker, L., Martin, D., Martin, M, Family factors in childhood obesity, (1986). *Amer. J. Fam. Ther.*, 14:247-253.

Hill, S.M., Milla, P.J., Colitis caused by allergy in infants, (1990). *Arch. Dis. Child.*, 65:132-140.

Malony, M.J., Klykylo, W.M, An overview of anorexia nervosa, bulimia, and obesity in children and adolescents, (1983). *J. Amer. Acad. Child Psychiat.*, 22:99-107.

Pollock, I., Warner, J.O, Effect of artificial food colours on childhood behaviour, (1990). *Arch. Dis. Child.*, 65:74-77.

Poskitt, E.M.E., Obese from infancy: a re-evaluation, (1980). *Top. Paediatr*, 2:81-89.

Rutter, M., Tizard, J., Whitmore, K. (Eds), *Education, Health and Behaviour*, Longman (1970). Reprinted 1981 by Robert Krieger Publishing, New York.

Shapiro, L.R., Crawford, P.B., Clark, M.J. *et al*, Obesity prognosis: a longitudinal study of children from age six months to 9 years. (1984). *Amer. J. Public Health*, 74:968-972.

Spence, S.H, Behavioural treatments of childhood obesity, (1986). *J. Child Psychol. Psychiat*. 27:447-453.

Stunkard, A.J., Sorensen, T.I.A, Hanis, C., Teasdale, T.W., Chakraborty, R., Schull, W.J., Schulsinger, F, An adoption study of human obesity, (1986). *New Engl. J. Med*. 314:193-198.

Zeisel, S.H, Dietary influences on neurotransmission, (1986). *Adv. Paediatr*., 33, 23-48.

FURTHER READING

Bender, Arnold, E. & Brooks, L.J. (Eds), *Body Weight Control: The Physiology, Clinical Treatment and Prevention of Obesity*, Longman (1987)
A very detailed and high-power book about obesity in adults but also relevant to young people.

Rutter, Michael (Ed.), *Scientific Foundations of Developmental Psychiatry*, Heinemann Medical Books (1980)
An excellent reference book on the wider aspects of child development.

Brostoff, Jonathan, Gamlin, L. *The Complete Guide to Food Allergy and Food Intolerance*, Bloomsbury (1989)
A useful and detailed book written for the lay public. Particularly helpful about the elimination diet.

Gilbert, Sara, *Tomorrow I'll Be Slim: The Psychology of Dieting*, Routledge (1989)
Written for adults but contains useful psychological information about dieting.

INDEX